Global TESOL

Teaching English to Speakers of Other Languages

An Orientation Guide

An orientation to the professional of TESOL
and a practical guide to developing and teaching courses and lessons
for English language learners locally or anywhere across the globe

**Teachers • Cross-cultural Trainers • Career Changers
Travelers • Au pairs • Interpreters • Translators**

Sarah Anne Shope, MAPW, MS Ed TESOL, PhD

Global TESOL
Teaching English to Speakers of Other Languages
All Rights Reserved.
Copyright © 2013 Sarah Anne Shope, MAPW, MS Ed TESOL, PhD
v2.0

Published by Globális Trend

ISBN: 978-0-578-11085-1

Library of Congress Control Number: 2012914620

PRINTED IN THE UNITED STATES OF AMERICA

CONTENTS

Preface: English in the Real World

Introduction: What in the World Are You Getting Yourself Into?

English in the Real World

Today more than ever, people are interested in multicultural issues. Learning and teaching language is a great way to get involved, whether for money, for the love of learning, on a volunteer basis, through community programs, industrial contract training, churches and schools, in the United States, or in another country. The following material is for the person who wants to be directly immersed in multiculturalism and to hone excellent skills in the art of language teaching. This guide is of great interest to global travelers; community, industrial, and human resource directors; social and political activists; faith-based organization leaders; and any individual engaged in cultural issues, the education of adults, or simply in making language accessible. This is a course of *attitude*, down-to-earth strategies for planning and teaching, tips for handling difficult situations, and ideas to spark your vision. By taking the mystique out of language learning and language teaching, this orientation guide opens a door for you to enter a rich new world by helping others acquire language.

Many people do not realize that the field of TESOL is wide open and there are few widely accepted standards for teachers of English to speakers of other languages (aside from kindergarten-through-twelfth-grade public-school systems). Though some English learning is done in public schools, much more learning takes place outside of academia, and the genuine standard is that of effectiveness, whereby people actually learn to use the language in a meaningful manner. After having taught people from nearly every country and on every level over decades, I have spent recent years instructing people from all walks of life in the basics of how hone a natural style of teaching while drawing from the human instinct for communication. That in itself is a worthy standard.

Universities may tell you that you need a particular degree in order to teach; however, in the real world, teaching happens on many levels. This guide is written so that you can use your desire to help your fellow humans and fortify yourself with confidence that you absolutely can do the job effectively. Though techniques and materials are essential and they are addressed in the following pages, more important are the two keys to good language teaching: 1) a grasp of the power of intrinsic motivation, and 2) skills in the facilitation of interactivity. Those two components drive the TESOL process. The only other element needed is a passion to help others.

If this is a new area of exploration, you will find much of what you need to move into the contemporary world of teaching *real* English to real people. Beginning teachers will learn techniques to organize classes, create meaningful lessons, and teach individuals or groups of people to use the language. If you have already been teaching, you will find new ideas and a fresh attitude toward the work. Even if you have been in education for eons, you will get new ideas and find the freedom to put aside any old ways that often do nothing more than create barriers to learning.

When instructors do not know the basics of real-life language learning, they have difficulty moving people ahead in the language. They may spend precious time talking, reading and explaining instructions, and assigning material; all the while, the act of learning to use the language is not necessarily taking place. The following units are packed with ideas, examples, and observations that can help you become a more effective instructor no matter what your background is and no matter in what situation you find yourself teaching. The units are presented in such a way that you can easily pick and choose techniques to get started and then come back to build on your skills after you have gotten your feet wet. This guide makes no get-rich-quick promises; nor does it suggest that you will become a revolutionary in the field of language, but it provides assurance that you will be able to take the material and use it on a sustained basis for a successful teaching.

Acknowledgments

Finally, a chance to put it in print, the very thing I wanted to say for so many years: Thank you, my dear students. You taught me well, and with such patience, and for so many years. In those fragile beginning years in California when it seemed none of us knew a lick about teaching people to speak English you came to America by boat, by plane, and sloshing through the water of a not-so-grand river to try to do the best that was in your power to make a life for yourself and your families. And in that time, you sat before me and smiled to encourage me when I taught well, and you urged me on when I struggled to teach anything at all. You pumped new blood into me, as you do into this country. You taught me what it means to be human, and you taught me to look into those eyes that I had never laid eyes on before. And you taught me how to pronounce your names properly out of respect, and to feel your cultures and your hearts. With tears I thank you, and as always, wish you the best for your lives. Yes, we were and are in the right places at the right times.

Also, I thank my TESOL students who continue to bring the world to me. I love your enthusiasm, your fresh desire to fix the world, and your patience and tolerance to let it be. We will keep trying to do both. Your pure and forthright love of humanity—it envelops and opens me. I appreciate your caring. And, thank you, Longstar, for the urging to make life such a gypsy adventure.

What in the World Are You Getting Yourself Into?

Say I'm ten years old. I know something and I know it well. Now approaching me on the sidewalk a few blocks from my home is the neighbor boy, my buddy, Dennis, whose mother has sent him off to the corner market to buy a pound of sliced beef. He doesn't know "the thing" that I know, and darned if I am going to share what I know with him. There is such power in confidential information, wouldn't you say? Let him stumble his way through his childhood without any extra advantages, any tidbits of wisdom, such as the fact that Cunningham's Market is closed today due to flu in the family. *Go ahead, Dennis,* I think to myself, *walk all the way to that corner.* Then I can smile later as I watch him wearily trod back in realization that he has just wasted his precious playtime. He could have been out in the backyard playing horse races with me, as we often did on those warm summer afternoons, on brooms whipped with our authentic jockey crops that seemed to make the brooms go faster. Surely my bit of exclusive information could have made that difference in Dennis' available time.

There is that side of us which, on occasion, gets egotistical pleasure from withholding information. And that child in me might say, *"Nah, nah, nah, nah, nah,* I know something you don't know." Yet there is that other side, that desire to impart information just because we know it. The caring, mature part of us says we owe it to people to tell them something that can make a difference in their lives: perhaps a difference in how they perceive the world, or a difference in their success and in their self-esteem. That is not about buying time to play horse races; it is about human compassion. And it is more than that. When we impart knowledge to someone else, it makes *us* feel good about ourselves. Fortunately, there is that part of our nature that finds far more pleasure in sharing information than in withholding it.

Even the trivia that we pick up here and there becomes a source of satisfaction as we tickle our brains and someone else's with it. Sometimes it is just the pleasure of communication or the silly game of playing with language that intrigues and entertains us. Then there is that great imparting of truly pertinent information (telling someone something that will truly make a difference to that person): how to strum a few chords on a guitar, how to open an attachment on an e-mail, how to properly punctuate a sentence, how to get a bargain on a purchase. When I look back on my life, that incident is perhaps the first evidence that I was a teacher, a natural teacher. I often tell students that I could easily teach zoology -- or anything, for that matter -- if I just knew the material. It is that fulfilling feeling of offering something of value to someone else, something that will benefit him or her. *That is teaching.*

Discovering that you are a teacher can come at various times in life. We find it and explore it as siblings, later as parents, and then again as we come into advisory or supervisory positions in our careers. I recall that I taught my younger sister to drive, back when our parents were busy with other things. That was a long time ago, but I did it and she and I own that experience. She doesn't call annually to thank me; nor can she hold me responsible for any of her fender-benders. I did it just because it was there to do and I could do it. Though I do recall feeling a bit of apprehension at the time, it was something I am happy I had the opportunity to do. *That's teaching.*

We are all teachers to some degree. All we need is opportunity. The desire may be there, but once we set a picture in our minds of our having the ability and confidence to teach, that desire will blossom. We may be many things in our lives, but we are all teachers. And we are all teachers of language, though few of us realize it. We all use and negotiate language on a regular basis. We are continuously acquiring new ways of communicating through language, and in turn we are imparting ideas to people around us. Yet some of us make a career or an avocation of teaching, or at least we take on an occasional task of instruction in conjunction with another career. The latter scenario is becoming more and common as people in industry and in the ministry find themselves working with non-English or limited-English speakers. So the door begins to open.

Who Are the Teachers of English to Speakers of Other Languages?

They are everywhere. They come from every conceivable background, career, level of training and academic foundation, and often from no academic training whatsoever. They are people just like you and me. They are all ages: some young, some old, and many in between.

How Do People Get into This Field?

For many who find themselves teaching people to speak English, it often came about as a fluke. Though there are academic degrees available that might lead individuals directly into TESOL (Teaching English to Speakers of Other Languages) or TEFL (Teaching English as a Foreign Language), most of the people I talk with have come out of other career preparation. Somewhere along the way they realized they wanted to teach and they were, for one reason or another, drawn to teaching internationals. Few are specifically attracted to the field because they want to deconstruct and reconstruct the English language; rather, people are enticed because they love working with people and learning about other cultures and languages. Or they slipped into a position of teaching purely out of economic need.

As silly as my personal story seems at this point in my life, I can tell you that it is not all that unique. There was a short time in my life when all I wanted to do was play tennis and drive around Southern California in a rather pricey car. Who knew that such a desire would lead me to a field that would change my life? I was simply looking for a part-time job to supplement my writing income. I had been dabbling in short fiction and article writing, and took on occasional writing and photography assignments. I knew I would have to do more to make the payments on my dream car, so I fought the traffic from my cushy little subdivision in Orange County and drove all the way to Los Angeles because I had heard a rumor that some folks up that way might be interested in learning English as a second language, or third, or fourth, or fifth language. Little did I know! Three hours after applying for an evening teaching job at one of the larger schools, I was standing in front of approximately 60 adults who couldn't say "boo" in English.

Funny story, yes—nonetheless, a true one. I was hired on the spot at an unexpectedly high hourly pay rate after a five-minute interrogation that clearly revealed I had no qualifications to do the job. The reason I was hired? The school desperately needed people to teach. I could speak the language (English, that is) and I had a car. I sensed that the fellow who hired me thought I would at least try to fulfill my promise to be there on time and leave the classroom free of debris upon ending each session. He did ask a little about my training and schooling. I had a bachelor of arts at that time, but I later found out that my undergraduate work (including my minor in English) was not at all pertinent to teaching people to speak the language; nor was it required for instruction on the adult level. I had no idea what I was getting myself into by taking a position in the heart of one of the most volatile multicultural areas in the United States, an atmosphere with which I was completely unfamiliar. Had I known the truth in the beginning, I might never have taken such a plunge. But by the time I was in over my head -- well, I was just that, and with no way out: I now had a huge car payment.

When I share my story with my current TESOL students, I tell it with great humor: how I battled through the first sessions of teaching with little or no teaching materials, and how I couldn't even figure out the nationality of my students. I could hardly ask them; they didn't speak English. But the punch line of the story is this: I survived to tell about it because those students gradually taught me how to teach. It took plenty of time and patience on their parts, but they worked on me over those first months, then -- it seemed -- they brought in replacements to push me through more semesters, then years, and on and on, through more than a decade. We all survived, and now I am here in hopes of cutting down your learning time by showing you the ropes from the get-go.

Many teachers come into the field through experiences similar to mine. They come with degrees in every possible field, and some sneak in without any post-high school studies. Some even get grandfathered into programs and become great teachers. Most, I would hope, go on to get some formal training for various reasons, but the real test of their teaching ability is one of reality: Do most of their students learn to use the language or not? Are many of their students motivated to continue, and do they enjoy the process enough to continue? Of course, teaching credentials can be necessary in some situations, and certifications look great, but the important proof of teaching skill is apparent in the accomplishments of the learners. That is one of the things I love best about teaching English to speakers of other languages: It's still a pure art.

Where are the jobs? At the risk of sounding redundant, the answer is the same: They are everywhere. The larger metropolitan areas have been running ESL/ESOL programs for decades. But something new is happening now throughout this country: The outskirts of the bigger cities are seeing more and more non-English or limited-English populations for a variety of reasons, partly because people are not feeling they need to confine themselves to the big cities such as Los Angeles, New York, Miami, Houston, and so forth; they—just like many second-, third-, fourth-, and fifth-generation folks—want to find the best living situations and job opportunities, even if it takes them into the suburbs and the countryside. Programs are cropping up everywhere: in industry, in community centers, through adult and continuing education programs, through missions and in churches, and through the efforts of entrepreneurs who intend to make a lucrative career from their skills, or who just need to make those car payments.

Take a closer look at those teachers. Who are they and where do they come from? For the most part they are people who, for one reason or another, have found that part of themselves that loves the process of learning and teaching—hardly separable processes. They generally have one thing in common: a desire to impart something that will be of value to another human being. Teaching English to speakers of other languages runs the gamut of situations and salaries. The pay can be wonderful (often a good hourly rate, or a considerable contract rate) or it can be nothing. If you are in a financial position to volunteer your time, the need is definitely there. Some programs have limited funds, perhaps enough to provide a classroom and some books, but nothing to offer an instructor. Some wonderful teaching is done on that basis. Many people, however, have to be reimbursed for their time, and the potential for earning money is unlimited -- or I should say, limited only by the instructor's abilities and his or her entrepreneurial skills.

Who Are Those Speakers of Other Languages in Need of English?

Opportunities for positions are everywhere that prospective students live and work. Sometimes speakers of other languages are concentrated near a large plant that hires people for their abilities to do certain jobs that do not require English proficiency. People come from all over the world to get jobs that will pull them and their families up and out of poverty. Those workers need to learn the language in order to move beyond those manual-labor positions. They will take classes offered by the employer, or they will attend any class they can find in the community. Those workers often bring with them spouses, parents, and children, and those family members need to know the language in order to survive in our society.

Students come to this country for more reasons than just economic; they come because loved ones brought them, or loved ones were already here; some people come to escape political situations or as refugees of war; or they come on a temporary basis because they can afford to spend time away from their homelands. Some go back home in time, and many stay on. They come in all ages, cultures, languages, and from all social and economic backgrounds and countries. Some are well-educated in their native language, and some are fluent in multiple languages. Some have advanced degrees and outstanding accomplishments, and some have nothing but a place to live, a bicycle, and a change of clothes. Some English learners are in their own countries, and for various reasons they recognize the importance of gaining skills in the language of money. Students and prospective students are everywhere, and they are from everywhere, yet they have one thing in common: They want to learn more English.

One of the great pleasures of teaching English to speakers of other languages is that it is a continuous learning experience for the teacher. The students bring so much from their cultures into the classroom that the teacher cannot help but be fed a daily dose of multicultural education.

The Benefits of Occasionally Falling Through the Cracks

It is important to get the kind of experience that will teach you how to be an effective teacher, and at the same time teach you about the field. My best advice is that you find some entry situation, and get in there and do your best to gain practical experience. You will figure out the *ropes* as you go, and your skills will develop naturally. Keep the important elements foremost in your mind: 1) work from intrinsic motivation, and 2) use interactivity. (Those elements are explained thoroughly in upcoming units.) Keep moving forward as opportunities arise. As you become involved with internationals, you will begin to see that there is a world fully developed around them, and learning English is a major component of that world. As people find out about you and your desire to teach, doors open wide.

It seems there is a solid division between people who have access to the English-speaking culture in the US and those who run head-on into a wall. There are, however, numerous cracks in the wall, and the ambitious, the industrious, and the lucky ones seem to find ways to get through. You become instrumental in that process because when they slip through the cracks, you are there to assist them as they struggle. I refer to the fact that a new person coming to the United States without the benefit of having already learned English usually must work long hours at low wages just to survive. That leaves little time for school. Yet, courses and complete programs crop up all around, due to people who push for them. Some are through community actions and faith-based organizations, and some are backed with federal money. Positions for instructors pop up quickly and you just happen to be there -- at the right place and time. Your students squeeze out precious time to attend your classes so that they can move up in their work situation and in their access to the community. Sometimes it seems as though they and you have—in a good way—simply fallen through the cracks of the educational system; yet if it were not so, those folks would not have a chance. Once the classes are going and people find out that you are actually teaching effectively, word spreads and others come to class. Word of mouth spreads rapidly when the need is strong. Your classes become a mix of people from various economic and social levels, including low-wage workers, isolated homemakers, affluent students, and academically-oriented and vocationally-motivated students.

If you decide to work in industry, or eventually go that direction because it can be so much more lucrative, you will want to make time to explore everything that is going on in the area. You can do that by talking to people. If you are teaching in a community center or through adult education, ask your students if there are any classes being held at their places of work. You will soon find out what is going on in your community and get clues as to where you might set your sights. When you feel you know enough about what's what, you can propose a class for a company. As you learn to teach well, you will most likely be asked to teach more classes. Get experience wherever and however you can, then build on that experience!

You might decide to travel to another country and teach for a year or so. It will serve you well to get as much experience as possible before you leave. That will help you to compete with other prospective teachers from North America, The United Kingdom, and other English-speaking countries where they've been trained in British schools. Find out everything you can about the country and the culture before you leave, then go for it. Try to get some teaching experience before you go, but don't allow your lack of experience to stop you from getting started. If you are a true teacher, that characteristic will come through no matter what obstacles are put in your way.

The Great Underground

Getting involved in teaching English to internationals changed my life dramatically. At first, it simply acted to immerse me into a world that had before seemed only a shadow of the culture in which I'd grown up. Then, in time I came to realize there was an extraordinarily rich inter-culture that had previously been quite elusive. Not only did I meet interesting students and teachers from every corner of the world, I was able to observe the intricacies of many cultures and become a part of intercultural dynamics. It fascinated me that people of varying cultures could interact so effectively, even when there were language barriers between them. Sometimes I saw cultural clashes, yet more often I was able to see how gracious people can be and how beautifully cultures and individuals can complement one another. I worked, and still do, with people of drastically different experiences; academic, educational, and professional levels; financial and social levels; and age differences. In addition to all that, I discovered that there is an entire society of teachers who give their energies to such cultural and life enrichments. How can that sort of experience not affect the teachers? Certainly I am not trying to say that those who teach English to speakers of other languages are any better than anyone else, but I will point out that they usually have lives with added texture, thus potential for heightened sensitivity to cultural and individual differences and to the larger world.

There is so much to learn and such good company to keep. At some point in your adventure into teaching, you may notice that what seemed to be an *underground* is actually the real world in microcosm. Once you have entered the world of teaching internationals, you may find that you are in a far more realistic place than the one that is closed off from people of other cultures and languages.

The Decision to Move Forward

It is important for you to make practical decisions. It may be that there is a situation, an opportunity in front of you, one that has drawn you to seek out this orientation guide and program; perhaps you know people who are already in the field of TESOL and you just have a feeling that it would be fun, or maybe someone has enticed you to take on a teaching project and you know you need to be brought up to speed on the subject. Whatever the lure, you will want to make an educated decision as to whether or not you should take the plunge. In addition to absorbing the material in this book, you will do well to search out some classroom situations and ask if you can observe. Check around the community for adult education, continuing education, or community centers that offer ESL classes. Or, if you are working for a sizable company, see if in-house classes are being run.

As you start investigating one situation, ask that instructor or students about other available classes. You will be surprised at how the underground begins to surface. There are so many opportunities out there, and if you don't find something that perfectly suits you, consider creating a program on your own or with a friend. Be careful, though, because before you know it you will be immersed in the teaching of English to internationals. Once it gets into your blood, you may have trouble walking away from it.

What Are the Tools You'll Need to Step Forward?

Two major things:

1) Understanding of the basics of language acquisition so that you can *develop an attitude* toward real-life teaching

2) Knowledge about how to put lessons together that will allow people to learn the language to their fullest capacities.

Those elements sound terribly complex, but by breaking them down into common components you can get the sort of grip on them that you will need to get going. Then, having that understanding and knowledge, along with the experience you will gain from teaching, will give you the foundation to do whatever comes your way. The units that follow are designed to give you that understanding and knowledge. Language acquisition is a huge field, which you can and might want to study for the rest of your life; nevertheless, what you need in the beginning is an investigation into how first language is acquired so that you can make a comparison of the natural language acquisition process with a more forced process of second-language learning. Getting some basics of the theories that have already been formulated and researched will allow you to understand why and how natural language learning is integral to effective teaching. Next you will want to dig more deeply to understand how the inner needs of the student play such a strong part in his or her learning and how you can take advantage of that intrinsic motivation to combine it with interactivity in a tutoring or classroom situation.

Once you begin to grasp those concepts, you will need to see how they work in action. That is why the fat Unit Three on teaching techniques and tools will be timely. Still, rather than learning a list of hard and fast rules on teaching, you will fare better by getting hold of the principles behind effective techniques and gaining an understanding of why certain tools work well and others can simply be time-wasters. (Therefore, it will not serve you well to skip over the upcoming chapters.) Also, you will appreciate having the list of life topics and the breakdown of levels of learning so that you won't need to spend precious time reinventing the wheel. You can then apply your personal creativity to those issues and use your resourcefulness to learn how to build interactive lessons. Your new knowledge will allow you to more instinctively break down barriers and set and meet goals that will have meaning for your students and for whoever is providing you with the opportunity to teach. You will have knowledge of how to put practically any curriculum together, and you will have a good sense of what you will need to do to establish and maintain a professional approach to your teaching so that it can grow in whatever direction you desire.

The material in this guide is designed to move you through your teaching experience, from the starting point of knowing you want to teach yet do not know how, to the place of effectively conducting classroom sessions with confidence and learning to accept the gratitude that will be bestowed on you as you help people with one of the most important facets of their lives, including the mastery of communication, and in a time when they are most fragile. What better gift to offer!

Use this guide as a continuous reference while you are planning lessons and organizing curriculum, and turn back to it when things feel a bit off-kilter. If you keep yourself grounded in the basics of intrinsic motivation, interactive lessons, use of a curriculum based on student and instructor goals, plus a heartfelt attitude of PC (polite consideration) for language and culture of all individuals, you will succeed.

Oh, and be sure to show up for class on time.
That will put you steps ahead of much of the world.

The Big Picture of Language Learning

In this unit:

- How We Learn Our First Language
- First Language Versus Additional Languages
- Language Acquisition Theory in a Nutshell
- Theories, Research, and Realities
- Integration of the Four Components of Language
- Sources of Motivation
- Academic Versus Vocational Approaches
- Your Knowledge of the Subject

How We Learn Our First Language

If you speak another language or you have learned even a little of another language, you will probably be thinking about how you did that and how successful or unsuccessful the language experience was. That exploration can take you to these questions: *How did you acquire your first language (thank Mom and Dad, or perhaps your grandparents)? What did your parents (or caretakers) do, and how did they do it and did they do a good job?*

In an orientation course for teachers of English to speakers of other languages, we take nearly a two-hour session to pick apart the four components of language in order to look closely at just how we acquired our first languages. I will take you through that enlightening process. In small groups of perhaps three or five people, the participants take one of the components (listening, speaking, reading, or writing) and thoroughly dissect it based on the question: How did you acquire the component in your first language, beginning in infancy then moving all the way through to the present time of your adulthood? Afterward, each group presents its findings. People share stories of how they think they came into listening, speaking, reading, and writing.

Though the anecdotes are different each time, the basics are always the same every time I teach the course. That little procedure requires us to look closely at what took place as we learned our first language, and it forces us to consider the roles of the four components of language. Our final discussion goes something like this: "What is the first component of language?" After a moment's hesitation someone says: "Listening." How subtly we learned to listen. Someone in the group is likely to digress, even to the womb, and remind us that as infants we learned to listen. Sounds began to take on certain meanings, and in early infancy we recognized that sounds were linked with objects, people, and feelings. If we hadn't acquired those listening skills early on, we would struggle with the speaking component -- as does a deaf child. We could spend an hour talking about listening and its various levels.

I wonder about listening because in my early years of teaching I pushed people to participate rather than to just sit there listening. Now, as I think about how much learning happens in the listening stage of first-language learning, I know that much learning actually does go on in the time that students are participating simply by listening. People participate in different ways. Some prefer to take in everything around them, and some focus on their own speech more than any other element. Most of us fall somewhere in the middle. It is all important learning time. Yes, listening is an activity and an acquired skill.

What then would you think is the second component of language? Ah yes, speaking! What I generally hear next from my group activity is something like, "I learned to speak my first language by identifying the things that interested me and the things I wanted." Simple identification! Then someone mentions learning some basic verb packages such as "gimme" and "me want." Aha, intrinsic motivation! A child needs to communicate in order to get what he or she wants. What a wonderful strategy the instructor must have put forth. And who was that instructor? . . . a parent, usually Mom with contributions from Dad and other family members. What we discover over and over again is that our parents, or whomever we got the rudiments of our first language from, did what they did instinctively. The participants of the TESOL course next go on to discuss just how they actually learned that first language: family conversations, television, the neighborhood, the bigger world, and, of course, school. It is now clear to us that listening and speaking are the first components of language to be learned, and they are closely intertwined.

How did the various levels of language structure build up? People are often amazed that they hadn't ever considered that question before. The process had been so natural; it just happened. We discover that we learned our first language tacitly and that no one actually set out to teach us the language on any particular levels. There were no textbooks or curricula. It all came through intrinsic motivation and plenty of interactivity, the key ingredients in language learning.

What is fascinating about our little language-component-dissection exercise is that the participants (all so different from one another) discover to a deeper degree the importance of individual differences in learning. Some admit that their verbal skills seemed stronger than their auditory skills, or vice versa. From this we recognize that within a group of adults such as the TESOL participants, there is a range of experiences and levels. That helps us to realize that in an ESL or EFL classroom there will be such diversity, and probably much more.

Then comes reading! How did you acquire your skills in that component of language? How did we learn to read? Most of my students of teaching recall that they learned to read in classrooms of children who were all approximately on the same level. And that issue opens up a new area, one of literacy in the first-language classroom versus the second-language classroom. Literacy is one of the strongest variables in a group of speakers of other languages. Sure, if everyone in the classroom were at the exact same level of literacy, we could simply toss them a text and move forward day by day at a smooth pace -- the utopian classroom that never does actually exist in the real world of teaching English to speakers of other languages. Not only are there fast readers and slower readers, there are those who prefer to read or simply dislike reading. And there are the non-readers, and the nearly illiterate. They are by no means the "dummies"; rather they are people who for numerous reasons have never had the opportunity to learn to read in their own language, or their literacy is extremely limited. Also, keep in mind that there are many bright people who simply do not pick up a second language easily.

Finally we take on the component of writing, and we question, how can writing possibly be separated from reading? My students who have dissected that component report back their childhood experiences of eking out the letters of the alphabet with fat crayons and pencils. Oh, those fine motor controls skills—just how did we acquire them so easily? How did we get through those early years of working with writing tools until the pencil would just fall into place in our hand and move like lightning across a page? Yet there are reports from the group about problems with writing: left-handedness and its old stigma, or switching from left to right and back again, the of lack of fine motor control for various reasons including the occasional broken finger or hand, plus all sorts of struggles with holding that skinny pencil. It all seemed so natural because we were so young and moldable, and the muscles of our hands developed along with the process.

Then what about the student of English who has never gone through the writing readiness stages, perhaps because he or she was busy working in that time rather than sitting in a classroom? Some older students have an extremely difficult time because they grew up with tools in their hands, and now as adults they can barely hold a pencil to scratch out their names. They simply didn't have a chance to develop those fine motor controls as they were acquiring their first language.

First Language Versus Additional Languages

While we cannot return to those wonderful natural steps of learning a "mother tongue," we can certainly draw much from investigating them. First, consider what is the most obvious method used when you learned your first language. You guessed right—it is repetition. "Say Daddy!" Does that sound familiar? How many times would you suppose little cues such as that were given to you? Yes, thousands of times you were prompted to practice words and phrases. That is the first big step in learning language: Practice hearing it and saying it, over and over again. The trick is simply one of utilizing the natural mimicking nature of a child. Though language acquisition is much more than simply mimicking, the technique transfers easily to an English-learning classroom. Teacher says, students repeat.

Look more closely at what takes place in the mimicking stage. "Say Daddy!" And what generally comes out of the child's mouth? "Da da." Sure. But with additional prompting from family members, the child learns to stretch "da da" into "daddee." There is the second big transferable technique, that of breaking the words into parts and practicing pronunciation. When a student attempts to master the sounds of the language, he or she must break the flow, separate out the sounds, isolate them, and practice, practice, practice. It all seems contrived in the classroom, but then it must be. Yet, it is amazing how easily a group of mature and sophisticated adults will join in the mimic and repeat drill, especially when there is so much at stake in learning English, and especially when the teacher makes it all seem so natural and acceptable. The instructor can quickly go to the basics of first-language learning and set up situations whereby the students can listen then speak, listen then speak, listen then speak—with no stress and pressure of reading and writing -- at least not yet.

The third transferable technique is just as easy. Remember when you learned those first words? Well, no; you probably don't remember. Perhaps now you will need to focus on observations of your children or someone else's children. How does the child come to know what something is, and how things associate? Where does the *translation* take place? How does the child attach meaning to sounds? The child wants a cookie and he learns to express his desire by first drawing from identification, then struggling to convey his feeling of desire. Once he realizes that relationship between Mommy holding out a cookie and saying "Want a cookie?" he makes the needed effort to string that *w* word together with *cookie*, and before you know it, Johnny is begging, "wan cookie, wan cookie." Or perhaps he picks up the *give* and comes out with a big old "gimme cookie." But what sort of translation is taking place? It is a very direct sort, from mind and sound and through intrinsic motivation and interactivity. If we could just bottle that! The point is that there is no translation from one language to another. It is total immersion into the target language, with no translation crutch.

One of the first questions people generally ask when they learn of my teaching experiences is, "How can you possibly know all those languages?" It is probably good that the question didn't occur to me when I first began teaching English, since my own knowledge of other languages was quite shaky. That is the beauty of teaching English --the primary issue of modern language acquisition is immersion, just as it is in first-language acquisition. Not only is translation not needed, it can in many ways slow down the learning process. I realize that we've now opened a rather controversial topic, but you needn't take issue with it yet. Just continue on your journey of learning the ins and outs of teaching and you will come to understand that immersion is a key technique to language learning and that it certainly takes a tremendous pressure off the teacher and the students once that knowledge sets in.

We can draw a lot from the lessons of first-language acquisition to create effective teaching techniques for learning second languages. The components of reading and writing came into first-language learning after those formative years of learning to listen and read. Yet we find ourselves trying to force all four components on our students at one time. That need not be. It is quite natural to begin with listening and speaking. The reading and writing will come later as the student has time and opportunity. What you will notice is that those with literacy will turn to the written word too quickly, while the less literate will find nothing but embarrassment over the issue. You can overcome those barriers for all concerned.

Language Acquisition Theory in a Nutshell

The following is not offered as a substitute for more thorough learning of the subject of theory, but to give you a bit of orientation to theory of language acquisition. There will come a time when your appetite is whetted enough to drive you to study more; however, to get started in the art of teaching English to students of other languages, you do not need more than the basics.

In 1880, in *The Art of Learning and Studying Foreign Language*, François Gouin described his observations about language teaching based on a personal experience. He had taken up the study of German while living in Hamburg for a year. His plan was to conquer the language by memorizing grammar and verbs rather than through conversing with native speakers. Though it took only ten days to complete his rote-memory task, he found he was still unable to understand German. He tried again, this time studying the roots of words and reinforcing his memorization of 248 verbs. Gouin continued by memorizing entire books, including a dictionary. But when he attempted to speak German, he was ridiculed for his pronunciation. Finally, after observing his young nephew who was acquiring his first language, Gouin decided the secrets to learning additional languages were in first-language acquisition. Gouin based his study on the following principle: Language is merely the representation of concepts, and its learning process is simply the act of transforming perception into conception.

Upon these ideas Gouin built his teaching techniques that formulate the Series Method. It was a straightforward method of teaching—no translating and no grammar rules -- and much more in line with natural language learning than anything that existed up to that point. He incorporated a series of connected sentences easily understood by the learner. For example: "I walk to the door. I draw near to the door. I draw nearer to the door. I get to the door. I stop at the door. I stretch out my arm. I take hold of the handle. I turn the handle. I open the door. I pull the door. The door moves. The door turns on its hinges. The door turns and turns. I open the door wide. I let go of the handle." (*L'art d'enseigner et d'étudier les langues*. Paris: Librairie Fischbacher)

This was a start. The Series Method helped language learners tackle vocabulary and word order as well as grammar. It seemed a realistic approach to learning, kindred to the natural way children learn. It was on this foundation that, a few years later, German Charles Berlitz devised his Direct Method, a teaching method which has become common to language learning.

Berlitz added the following ingredients:

• verbal activities
• spontaneous speaking, with absolutely no translation or grammar
• lessons taught in the target language only
• using everyday vocabulary and sentence structure
• verbal skills are built up gradually through question and answer techniques
• grammar as an integral part of the lessons with oral models presented first
• visuals used for vocabulary and idea associations
• speaking and listening are taught together
• pronunciation and grammar corrected as needed

Berlitz's Direct Method was becoming the most accepted and popular method of teaching language. Yet, due to public education's inability to incorporate it easily into the curriculum, there was and sometimes continues to be an ongoing tug-of-war between the older memorization method and the more modern Direct Method. While some of the aspects of the Direct Method are questioned by some theories and research, the primary elements of it are used continuously in public and private language learning situations.

Theories, Research, and Realities

Much research has been conducted and modern theories have evolved out of the study of first language, ranging from behaviorist to nativist to functional. By looking at language from an ethnographic viewpoint, researchers have produced theories that recommend whole (holistic) learning with interactive teaching/learning experiences. A study of language acquisition covers issues such as nature versus nurture and grammatical universals in language (word order, negation, verbs and nouns, questions, etc.), and then to focus on the relationship between language and thought processes -- an area difficult to approach in a scientific manner. In spite of all the research and never-ending discussions, imitation/practice often becomes the common avenue for second-language learning, and practitioners are most frequently attracted to a competence/performance approach because of funding restrictions and because results are easier to measure.

Some rather interesting neurological questions arise as we compare the acquisition of first and second language:

- Is there a time in a human's life when language acquisition no longer exists?

- How is language handled in the left versus the right hemisphere of the brain?

- Does this lateralization alter at different stages of life?

- What happens with language between ages two and puberty?

- Why do learners tend to retain accents when language is acquired after puberty?

There are psychomotor considerations related to "speech muscles" (again accents), and cognitive considerations that touch on the intellectual development of second-language learners. And there are issues of emotions—affective considerations. This becomes extremely important to teachers of English because students are often in a flux of anxiety and altering of attitudes. Some are particularly extroverted or introverted, or even extremely inhibited. Self-respect plays into language acquisition, as does peer pressure. As a teacher gains experience, he or she gains a deeper understanding of how language is intertwined with culture, and how important both are to self-esteem.

In the art of language teaching, teachers often develop their own methods in which they break down the language and present it in parts for students to memorize and absorb. But if care is not taken, such a technique can easily take the learning process away from more natural approaches, thereby weakening it.

Integration of the Four Components of Language

Combining the basic communication skills into *complete language* is often promoted in education, and such an approach needs to be handled with care and with enough flexibility to be inspiring and effective for the learner. Many instructors find themselves struggling with teaching materials, particularly assignment instructions, that do not suit their students' literary levels, and the students easily become frustrated, then discouraged. In first-language acquisition there is naturally a sizable time-gap between the oral and written components. Some learners begin speaking long before tackling reading and writing. Yet, educators begin planning lessons while somehow assuming that the adult student of English as a second language has already fairly well caught up to the literacy skills of his or her first language and can easily integrate listening, speaking, reading, and writing. While it is true that some can, the teacher quickly discovers that many cannot. These students desperately need to focus on listening and verbalizing just to break through the language, and then later they can tackle reading and writing exercises as their skills develop and as time permits.

When designing a course from a competency-based approach, it would seem that written language simply goes hand-in-hand with speaking and reading, especially on the lower levels: See the word, say the word, write the word. But what happens as the student moves up through the levels? Even many first-language English speakers would have difficulty with many of the advanced level ESL materials, especially if their earlier energies were concentrated in vocational areas rather than academics. How then can educators expect an individual to be interested in the academics of the language when all he or she wants to do is get a job as quickly as possible? On the other hand, does the more academically oriented student soon become bored with only conversational and competency-based courses? The key to this balancing act is always to have your teaching approach arise from the students' interests, goals, and levels.

Many texts use theme-based materials with real-life content. Often these topics are interesting and exciting to all levels of learners -- perhaps more so to middle and higher levels -- depending on their comprehension levels. Stories can involve true-to-life individuals or dramatic movie-like characters. They can cover a gamut of issues and events: contemporary, historical or a mix of both, many relevant to everyday life. No matter how exciting the content, it still must drive the student closer to his or her goals, and it should allow the less-literate student to move forward without embarrassment.

In any class, a discussion can take place between instructor and students before a reading assignment is handed out. An oral reading of the assignment can help to build listening skills; then a concentration on reading comprehension and reading techniques can assist in developing reading skills. Next, a writing component can be added easily by having students reconstruct or paraphrase sentences and sections of the reading. The thought to keep in mind at all times in relation to *whole language* is that a student never needs to be embarrassed, frustrated, or discouraged over problems with one component of language to the point that he or she cannot build on the components that come more easily.

Sources of Motivation

At any time when you are working with humans, you automatically will be a student of human nature and of various personalities. While you needn't spend time dissecting the human mind, you surely will find yourself fascinated by what is easily observable. It is simple: we love to learn—well, certain things anyway. But when we are truly inwardly motivated, we dearly love to learn. Perhaps you can recall spending hours on what could have been considered a task, yet in that time it was pure ecstasy. The time sped by and you were totally involved in the learning process because it just felt good. There was some sort of intrinsic motivation going on, though you likely didn't think about it at the time. That learning process was meeting some inner need, either due to the pleasure of discovery or the need to understand something. In any case, it was a great learning experience.

You can probably recall those times when someone else, for any number of reasons, wanted you to learn something. You learned it, willingly or begrudgingly. The motivation, however, was clearly coming from the outside. Compare the two scenarios, and consider which allowed for the more natural learning experience. Surely you've thought first about the intrinsically motivated one, but you cannot totally discount all extrinsic ones either. There are times when a good instructor needs to motivate the learner, and even more times when he or she simply needs to provide and facilitate opportunities for the learner to invoke his or her internal drive. This is an area for your creativity to kick in. You will find yourself enjoying the motivation process.

Academic Versus Vocational Approaches

There comes a time of separating the competency-based materials and classes from the more academic and grammar-based approach. In that time, some students begin to find their ways to university classes, where they are more thoroughly tested and often placed in upgrading classes. The *not-so-academic* students frequently struggle with language deficiencies throughout their lives. An instructor can play a role in the future of every student by supplementing competency-based lessons with enrichment materials, and involving students in lifelong reading and learning. It becomes important not to stereotype people, not to draw a line between academic and vocational "types" of students, but to become a resource person for each student's individual education track, formal or informal. We need to view students as having potential for great things, in the realm of higher academic education and technical and vocational expertise.

Your Knowledge of the Subject

This can be a major point of contention in the field of teaching people to speak English until we look at it closely. An instructor should certainly have knowledge of the subject he or she is presenting in a given course and in each lesson, although he or she cannot be expected to know everything there is to know about the English language.

Exactly what does the teacher need to know?

We assume that a person planning to teach English can speak English. Yet, most of us have interesting little quirks in our speech patterns: regionalisms, colloquialisms, slang, and occasionally some weak or incorrect grammar, or simply a lack of confidence in our knowledge of grammar. Usually we are semi-aware of the problems, but we do nothing to fix them since we feel that we are able to communicate well enough, or we just don't know how to remediate ourselves. Once a person gets face to face with material that is set up to teach the language, he or she runs into some conflicts. Those are not things to be terribly concerned about because we correct most problems as we go along. Our grammar usage becomes more precise as we drill our students in certain sentence structures. We often learn to correct our spelling of those tricky words that we struggled with when we were in school. Much of that learning takes place as we teach, and often just at the moment when we begin to teach a section of material.

Then, what else do we need? The instructor finds out what more he or she needs to know soon enough once the books are opened. There is a ton of terminology related to grammar and the structure of the language. Some of it is familiar to most speakers of

English (such as nouns, verbs, adjectives, and adverbs); however, some of it can throw off the most educated of folk (such as the conjugation of the subjunctive). Oh my, now we've hit on a dreadfully fearful subject: our knowledge of the workings of the language we speak. Even those fine folks with degrees in English often feel a tremor when the subject comes up. Though they studied long hard hours to earn their degrees, most of the material was in literature and composition. People often move away from any grammar terminology in their early years unless they are preparing to teach English grammar.

Remember that this material is written to dispel all the fears of teaching people to speak English, and we certainly won't shy away from this one. We will approach it in the most practical way, to make it digestible for any instructor from any walk of life. What exactly are the elements of language structure and grammar that we need to know, and when do we need to know them?

First of all, you can begin by getting hold of a good set of course books (texts) and look closely at the lessons and at the language terminology used in them. In the beginning levels you will see terms such as *simple present tense, present continuous, possessive adjectives*, and so forth. Look at the lessons and at how the concepts are revealed. If it is not familiar to you, it will become so rather quickly. What is the different between simple present and present continuous tenses? *Every day I study English. I am studying English now.* Aha! It's that easy! You already know that every day relates to the frequency of the action. *Every day I study English* is in simple present tense. But when we think about doing the action now, we use present continuous: *I am studying now.* The texts are designed to teach that concept to the student, so surely they are written in such a way that the instructor will pick it up quickly. If not, then I strongly recommend finding a better text. The textbooks will move you through nearly all of the building blocks of language structure; they will familiarize you with the necessary terminology as you go along.

Occasionally a teacher will get derailed in a lesson simply because a text uses an alternate term for an element of grammar: such as *present progressive* for *present continuous*. The instructor quickly realizes that those terms are the same. Sometimes students pick up terminology from one instructor and carry it into the class of another instructor who is not familiar with the term. There can be a feeling of "ignorance" on the instructor's part for a moment until that instructor realizes what the student is referring to. We learn quickly to cover ourselves with remarks such as "Oh, that's an interesting term," and move on without hesitation.

On the beginning levels much time is spent building vocabulary with simple sentence structures; therefore, you can stay afloat by simply reviewing the material you intend to teach. If anything is new, you will have time to think it through and look up any unfamiliar terms. Your success will depend on your ability to facilitate learning for adults who are struggling with the sound system and basic identification. Many instructors become specialist in the survival and beginning levels because they acquire skills in motivating people to continue when learning is most difficult.

If you are assigned to an advanced level, you will have a different set of challenges. Not only will you need to learn the necessary terminology, you will need to be sure you understand how the most complex structures work within the language. Again, a good text will help you greatly. Just learn to stay ahead. Often students will push ahead of a lesson by asking questions that involve new terms and concepts. That will spur you on to doing a thorough study on your own. Does it sound scary yet? Just consider this: The worst thing that can happen is that you will strengthen your own control of the language. It will not only affect how well you teach, it will enhance your speaking and writing abilities—a sort of a fringe benefit.

**Take the attitude that this is an adventure in communication
—a fascinating study in human nature and language arts.**

At the Heart of the Natural Learning Experience

In this unit:

- The Deepest of Drives
- Tapping Intrinsic Motivation Makes for Good Teaching
- Life Topics and Whole Language
- Recycling
- Building Blocks
- Movement and the Mind
- Interactivity and Great Learning
- Zen and the Art of Learning Anything

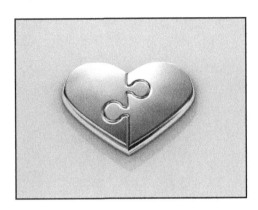

The Deepest of Drives

We learn most beautifully and most naturally when we want to learn, when it feels good and right to learn, when we need to learn in order to carry on -- and at the heart of that process is our inner (intrinsic) motivation. It is inborn, essential, peculiar, and natural. It is exhilarating and solacing. It is the deeper force that consoles us and encourages us to move forward. Without it, we only plod along through unawareness.

> **What an incredible thing,**
> **this nearly unidentifiable phenomenon,**
> **this ultra-natural procedure,**
> **this process at the base of nearly every inch**
> **of our being, this fundamental drive**
> **that leads us to the ways in which we learn—**
> **it is that inner urge that keeps us vital.**

Now that you recall your own first-language learning, or at least what you can remember of it, you also have memories of those magical moments of learning as you worked to gain competency at some communication arts skill: maybe a school paper, reading assignment, or the completion of a book that mesmerized you. If those images are vague, try remembering the times when you found yourself fully involved in any form of discovery. Your learning capacity felt infinite, truly limitless, and often the only thing that interrupted you was fatigue or hunger. There is great joy in exploration, and language acquisition can fall right into that experience. Students of English can come into class and become totally absorbed in the process, or they can sit there painstakingly forcing themselves to master some arbitrary rules and regulation of grammar. Often the difference lies in the instructor's attitude and his or her understanding of how to tap that inner drive to promote inner motivation.

Tapping Intrinsic Motivation Allows for Good Teaching

Do you remember the definition (or explanation) of intrinsic motivation from Unit One? ". . . meeting some inner need, either due to the pleasure of discovery or the need to understand something. In any case, it was a great learning experience." If intrinsic motivation is the basic ingredient in all of your lesson planning, you will do well. The byproduct is that your students will have a great experience under your teaching. So now comes your test question: How do we tap this inner drive and incorporate such motivation into each and every session?

It's easy! We work much in the same way our parents or first-language caregiver did: We identify what is of interest to the learner, what is important to him or her. That's very basic. We build our lessons on the topics of life, those that relate to the here and now. *But wait just a minute,* you say. *Every student is different, has different interests and needs.* Sure they do. Yet there are those common topics that we can build on, to move into the areas of individual interests. We simply move from the core of the students' interests and add in that which we know the student needs to learn.

Each lesson is then a combination of intrinsic and extrinsic motivation, yet it all evolves out of the intrinsic. The instructor learns to recognize the inner drive (intrinsic motivation) and then uses that to set up instructor-driven (extrinsically motivated) activities. Students want to learn, they remain engaged, and therefore they cannot help but learn. The classroom situation can create a continuous tapping of intrinsic motivation as the facilitator promotes a questioning (as opposed to interrogating) atmosphere. As new words and structures are learned, new questions immediately arise. As soon as the survival-level students master the basic colors, the various shades can be introduced. Students always want to know more, and the teacher can prod any situation for more "taps." A student wants to ask more questions, and therefore must learn more question structures in order to ask. Good teaching is a continuous tapping of that magical intrinsic motivation, and that fact is clearly evident in good facilitation of language acquisition.

Life Topics and Whole Language

Nearly every course begins with introductions of some sort and then moves into the areas of familiarity such as the school or place where the course is being held, family members and relationship terminology (*mother, father, grandparents, children*, etc.) friends and associations. These are things everyone has in common, and such discussions can act as ice-breakers. We all know it is common for people to ask about one another's family, and to take a conversation to an even friendlier level we often ask someone if he or she has children or siblings. The topic of family is generally great for starters, and it is always a good ice-breaker. The problem with this topic is the overuse of it. Often an instructor will have such a warm feeling of success with it that he or she will be inclined to return to it when other topics seem shakier.

Consider the learners: While they may enjoy talking about family to some degree, enough is enough, and they will be anxious to move on to other topics quickly. People and places are all around you, and your students are interested in such topics of real life. The people who work in and around your location are great for developing descriptive vocabulary. Identifying places that students frequent (stores, banks, post offices, libraries, and any commercial businesses and buildings) will be of interest. It is easy then to slide right into directions around the area and conversation about how to give and follow directions. ("Please tell me how to get to the post office.") That leads easily to all sorts of information exchanges and the general sharing of news.

Certain topics are vital to people who've recently relocated. Housing issues require many lessons, not only get vocabulary, but to acquire communication skills that will enable the speaker to protect his or her rights concerning such a thing. Many people new to this country will seek out stores where they can buy familiar foods, and those stores often employ people who can speak to customers in their native tongue; however, everyone wants the option to shop wherever the best selections and prices can be found. No one wants to be limited because of language. Students of English not only need to learn vocabulary of food, but the jargon of shopping (paper or plastic, credit or debit?).

Remember that basic identification of people, places, and things is always the foundation, the survival level. Then learners are ready to move into more complex structures, concepts, and associations.

Take a look at the following list of life topics and consider how many levels there might be to each one:

introductions	work
school, family and friends	health and emergencies
people and places	shopping
directions around the area	personal finances
sharing news and information	rules and regulations
housing	recreation
opinions	language strategies

Here is a sample of recycling a topic:

Personal Finances

currency $$$$

opening checking account

completing financial forms

counting & making change

opening saving accounts

filing tax returns

investing funds

Recycling

Now take another close look back at how you learned your first language. You recycled until it stuck. I'm sure I did, though I hadn't even thought about it in such a way until I began to seriously wonder how it was that people learn language.

I remember that I sat for hours in a classroom studying German, but later could recall only the words that I related to at that particular time: *teacher, student, classroom, book pencil*, and those interactive greetings: *Hello, my name is Sarah. This is my friend Wilhelm*, and so forth. Within the life topics there is a wealth of lesson material.

Any comprehensive ESL text series will supply you with such lessons. And your students will direct you in their specific needs if you allow them to do so. It is natural to begin with introductions *(Hello, Mr. Baker. My name is Carlos Ruiz.)*; though, again as with family topics, I suggest you don't overdo it. I have observed classrooms where the entirety of the first few lessons was taken up by introductions. Surely it will take time for the students to become acquainted with one another, learn how to pronounce names and how to do polite greetings. They perfect those introductions in time, but the first lesson must reveal to the students that you intend to move through plenty of pertinent material; therefore, it is important to give them a taste of what's to come. Spend a period of time in the first session introducing; then move into another lesson. Do so again the next lesson, then the next, until the basic introductions are mastered. Bring the topic back in to later lessons by building on those basics. *Hello, Mr. Baker. My name is Carlos Ruiz, and I'm here to speak with you about the position you advertised in the trade journal.* Recycling forces the creation of building blocks.

Building Blocks

Move quickly into topics of school, family and friends, people and places. The issues must be personalized to the student, and that is the easy part. Relate the lessons to the students' family members and their friends, here and at home. The places are those in your community, along with directions on how to get there and what to do there:

places such as the post office, the bank, the market, the department of motor vehicles, the library. Establish the basic vocabulary so that when you return to the topics, your students will be able to refresh their memories quickly and then build on those basics.

Sharing news and information can be a daily activity with text-based conversations as back-up. There is an abundance of great text available for guidance, but the sharing should be as personal as possible without, of course, going into areas that are too delicate for discussion. Housing, food, and work topics will beg for attention because these are areas that your students are dealing with on a daily basis. It is fine to add in mention of beautiful homes in wealthy neighborhoods, the finest of cuisine, and executive positions, but the base of lessons must be about the homes in local neighborhood, local restaurants and ethnic foods, local markets, and accessible jobs. You will want to build on discussion of homes and occupations in the students' homelands, and always zero in on what is truly of interest to the participants. At first you will have to do a bit of guesswork, but it doesn't take long until the students become just verbal enough to express something of their interests. Remember that you are working in steps, building blocks -- or shall we say, in layers. Lay the foundation and then build on it. You can take much of the guesswork out of your planning.

Though your students may be limited in language skills at this point, they still have to function in the community and with the community. Their first outreaches are usually through health and emergency services. Basic medical issues can be addressed on the beginning levels through identification of pertinent vocabulary: body parts, ailments, procedures, filling out forms, asking for medications or emergency assistance, and related telephone skills for setting and canceling appointments. Getting around in a grocery store or department store is important, as is personal banking. Students want to know how to ask for specific items (food, clothing, accessories), and they want to do so effectively and politely within the community's cultural standards. They need to know how to open bank accounts, write checks, how to read bills, and all the issues related to personal finances. They need basic vocabulary and then conversations and exercises that build on that word-stock.

Rules and regulations are of particular concern and require extensive discussion for clarity and reasoning. Students cannot easily take in all the requirements of a new culture, but there are some they need to know almost immediately in order to function effectively. They also have rights and responsibilities that may differ from those in their homelands. These topics need to be dealt with on every level, from survival through advanced instruction -- without giving legal advice. And it is never the same old things again and again; the topics are practically inexhaustible when you take a recycling and block-building attitude.

Recreation can be presented along with nearly any other subject, but it seems to work well with the topic of *opinions* because it allows students to discuss their preferences without any terribly threatening controversy. Trust me; it is far safer ground for opinions than politics, sex, or religion. Some language skills are specific to voicing opinion and blend nicely with skills for polite social conversation; thus, recreation is perfect for starters. Later you will build on those skills. Strategies for making effective communication jump onto the scene. How do you ask questions that allow for healthy discussion?

How do you use language to get what you want rather than just getting you a slap in the face? How do you make yourself heard and understood in the local culture? The English language can be tricky. We are so accustomed to saying things a certain way that we are often not even aware of the strategy behind our selection of words or our sentence structure. I remember my ESL students sometimes telling me, "I will not come to school tomorrow because I'm too busy." Nothing wrong with the sentence structure! But how much better the following statement is received: "I won't be able to come to school tomorrow because I have some business to take care of." There are some texts that deal directly with language strategies, and some that take it for granted. Many more ideas will come to you as you teach. Always work with the basics and then build on those.

Much more will come to you as you teach! This book offers guidance in how to move your students into topics and issues that will tap their intrinsic motivation, but the students will be the ones to show you the way. As you continue teaching, you will see that the steps are always right in front of you. Of course it would be nice if you could stay at least one step ahead of your students on some things, but don't count on that always happening. There will be times when you will dive into a lesson and they will beg for answers that are beyond your current understanding of the topic information or language structure, but *please* do not let that scare you. Just practice a little disclaimer that will get you through any situation: "That is a good question. Thank you for asking. We will talk more about it later." *Later* can be tomorrow or next week, depending on how long it will take you to come up to speed. But you needn't totally reveal your ignorance. And when you find yourself in that situation, remember -- we've all been there, time and again. The important thing is that you addressed the person's question. Be sure to follow up.

Movement and the Mind

In many cases we learn by repetition. *Cookie, gimme cookie. Gimme a cookie! Give me a cookie! May I please have a cookie?* And your students progress in the same way. *This is a book. There are books? Repeat after me! How many books are there? Three books. Please bring me three books!* Suddenly, through that command for physical reaction, we have moved into another realm of memory reinforcement. When a student sees you carry three books to another person, then hand them to him or her, that learner has more to work with as a frame of reference. If you then ask that recipient to take those three books to that learner, more reinforcement takes place. Now, go a step further and ask that learner to bring the three books to you. The participant is required to stand up, walk over to you, and hand you one, two, three books. The words to speak in that time become a part of the memory strengthened by the learner's movement. Movement can be an important part of each learning session. You will learn to incorporate it in ways that not only foster memory, but break the monotony of sitting in one place for a block of time. We will look at this even closer in Unit Three under "Total Physical Response (TPR)." But for now, just keep in mind that movement can be reinforcement for memory. Movement requires involvement, and involvement aids memory.

Interactivity and Great Learning

Close your eyes and envision a classroom. What do you see? Okay, let's get more specific. Let's say it is a history class, or perhaps science. Where is the teacher, and where are the students? Your reply, of course, will depend upon the types of classes you've attended or taught, if you've had such experience. But we most often associate teaching with the traditional lecture-style classroom wherein the teacher is at the front of the room and the students are sitting in rows facing the teacher. The teacher is imparting information, and students are, we hope, listening and taking notes. That set-up has served education well for centuries; yet many teachers have moved away from it, finding that they can hold their students' attention better by keeping them involved.

Some excellent teachers are able to engage the entire class even while using the lecture format simply because they make each student feel as though he or she is in a direct conversation with the teacher. Can you now envision such a classroom? The students are not sitting there passively; they are in an interactive mode, as though they might be called on at any moment. There might be a bit of tension, but the instructor has managed to involve nearly everyone and has somehow broken down the barrier between teacher and students. How much more meaningful the instruction becomes when the teacher can do that -- and it is not all that difficult. Now let's go even a step further and envision a classroom where the teacher is not glued into that position at the front of the room. It might be difficult to see who is the "head honcho," because the focus point is continuously moving. Though the teacher will often take the lead, any student can become the main speaker at any time. Now we can see more teacher-to-student interactivity.

Keep the vision alive and look closely at who is now interacting with whom. Perhaps a student is starting a conversation and another student is replying; then that second student moves on to engage yet another student. We see student-to-student interactivity. But can anyone and everyone be permitted to talk at once? Well, almost. Naturally it would become rather chaotic if that were the total picture; however, with effective facilitation, the entire classroom can move from teacher-to-students lecture, to teacher-to-student interactivity, to student-to-students interactivity, to student-to-student interactivity. Yes, active and interactive conversation. Isn't *talking* obviously a primary goal of any language-acquisition situation? The goal is to use the language, to interact one with another and with others, in order to become more comfortable with the language. The teacher then becomes the facilitator of the interactivity—another key to successful teaching.

Zen and the Art of Learning Anything

An uncle used to say, "The harder I try the worser it gets." But I never worried about him because I knew that he read a lot and was bound to stumble over the classic writing based on a fine ancient Eastern philosophical doctrine -- that book entitled *Zen and the Art of Motorcycle Maintenance*. Surely a study such as that would take anyone to the place of "Stop trying so darn hard and just let your mind give in to it," whatever *it* is.

Zen teaches that every separate thing exists in relation of one to another, and a thorough study of the discipline could lead one to sit quietly and contemplate how things are without making a forced effort to grasp it. Somehow it comes to us eventually, maybe. Odd as it might sound in relation to language acquisition, you will be pleasantly surprised to find that many learners will take just such an approach. They will simply sit there and take it all in, and to your astonishment, one day a meditating student might open his or her mouth and complete articulate sentences will flow from it. Amazing? Yes! Therefore we must always be aware that there is that level at which we can all benefit from listening. So, don't worry yourself gray because some students seem to be in a bit of a trance. Perhaps they are taking the high road and freeing their mind so that they might attain a *no-mind* receptive state wherein language can come in its most natural way. (But if by chance they nod off, then you can be fairly sure you have lulled them into a deep sleep.)

As you teach and as your students learn, everyone gains more language awareness. The process is largely intuitive, yet at some point you begin to get more grounded in the linguistic form -- the sound system, the grammatical make-up, and the lexicon (words and their meanings) -- of the English language. You can make a lifelong study of these subjects, self-directed or through formal courses, and that knowledge can add to your teaching skills. Just keep in mind always that such knowledge is an aid, while the students' intrinsic motivation and the interactivity with the language is what is most at the heart of your work. Don't let a love for phonology take you far from the real work of teaching the language in ways that matter to your students. With that in mind you can surely enjoy a healthy look at linguistics and phonology.

Such a study helps you to look at grammar in both descriptive and prescriptive manners, at morphology (the structure and form of word), syntax (the rules of sentence structure), word classes, and grammatical terminology. You digest much of the terminology as you go, a little at a time, as you study for and prepare lessons. You learn much about the sound system as you do pronunciation drills and notice the patterns of syllable, word and sentences stresses, the rhythms and intonations, and the phonemes (the minutest sounds of vowels, diphthongs, consonants, vowel reduction, and consonant clusters). Often the most stimulating study is that of mental lexicon: the meanings of individual words, phrases, compounds, idioms, metaphors, collocations, and the relationships of synonyms, antonyms and homonyms, connotations, and the differences between written and spoken English. Zen is a state of mind, a state of consciousness wherein we do not look at the elements of an entity as separate things; they exist only in relation to one another. When we teach, the so-called issues and elements of teaching become one. In fact, we can easily come to understand that there is no separation between those issues and elements and our students; and then a step further and we see that we too are *one with the entire process*. You are not "just a teacher," you are a part of the process of other human beings acquiring language in the most natural possible way within your circumstances. It is then difficult to make arbitrary decision outside of that unity, and your intuition is the best guide.

Your intuition will keep you focused on the students' inner needs to learn and accomplish. Intrinsic motivation is at the heart of learning anything, and it is the best ingredient for teaching language effectively and as quickly as possible. When participants need and want to express themselves, they will draw on the deepest of energy to try. Desire is a great driver! Keep it alive in every aspect of your classroom activities. When you see that your learners are fading, quickly change gears and move into areas that spark their desire to speak, to ask or answer, to communicate. We all have within us a strong need to express our deepest feelings. In various levels of instruction, the skills are not yet there to accomplish full expression, and frustrations can come quickly. Keep your mind and heart on the pulse of the group and help them to glide around those obstacles to communication. When the frustrations arise, back off and try coming in another door --quickly. There are so many topics to build lessons on; you will never run out of escape subjects to use when the going gets rough.

And interactivity is the element that makes it fun. *Just do it.* The admonition applies to anything that we might want to do, but some people easily become laden with concerns about performance over the activity. If you could *just do it* without the anxiety, you would have a far better chance at success. The pure enjoyment of interacting with others in safe yet invigorating circumstances makes the task less burdensome. We can forget for a while that much depends on acquiring the language, and in that challenging and comfortable classroom time we can feel somewhat the kid again. How great it would be if all learning were that way.

Teaching Techniques and Tools

In this unit:

- What Does and Doesn't Work Well
- Pre-testing and Figuring Out Where to Start
- Total Physical Response
- Drills and Repetitions
- Pronunciation
- Models and Change-outs
- Presentation, Practice, and Performance
- Incorporating and Ignoring Grammar
- Teacher-to-students and Student-to-student Interactivity
- Games and Other Silly Things
- Student-originated Teaching Tools
- Instructor-made and Store-bought Materials
- Levels and Topics
- Moving Conversations Forward While Holding Back the Reins
- Survival Kit

What Does and Doesn't Work Well

This unit is about how to choose and use techniques and tools based on how your students respond and learn. Over time you will discover that some techniques and materials work better than others under certain conditions; but you can save yourself plenty of time and save your students lots of grief by simply getting to know them, their needs and interests, and by doing everything possible to put yourself in their place. Then, all you need to do is build on the techniques and materials that work.

It is not be terribly difficult to find out what doesn't work, because your students let you know, often in non-verbal ways: constant looks of frustration, signs of boredom or of too much information too fast, indications that they are feeling humiliation or that you are teaching far over their heads, or worst of all through non-attendance. (Please don't ever jump to the conclusion that students' erratic attendance or drop-out rate is a direct reflection on your teaching. Irregular attendance is often a part of the business of teaching English to people who are in flux and often on the move, changing jobs, moving for any one of dozens of reasons, or simply getting discouraged over the challenge of assimilation. It is often a heck of a lot easier just to stay home.) Over time you will learn to recognize those elements and not feel bad about the inconsistencies of attendance. When you sense that student numbers are dwindling due to your inadequacies, you will feel bad. That's the time to take drastic steps to acquire new, more effective teaching techniques -- the sooner the better. However, it is those looks of frustration and bewilderment or boredom that act as daily cues to ineffective teaching techniques or materials. Sometimes the selection of techniques is based on trial and error.

You may find a technique that feels right for you and it may work beautifully for a particular group of students; then suddenly you have a new group and your tried-and-true technique just seems to fizzle. Your natural tendency will be to modify the technique, and modify and modify until it is no longer recognizable as your original technique. And that's fine – perfect, in fact. You will, however, want to be prepared to change gears quickly when you feel the ship beginning to sink. Say, for example, you are working with a nice group of young Mexican men ages 18 to 22 in the evenings (not an uncommon class situation). You may have watched another teacher use a certain teaching strategy in a morning class that was made up of older Asian students, and you decided to try it with your group. Mind you, this is not an attempt to stereotype young Mexican guys or older Asians, but there are generally some inherent age and culture differences. The Mexican guys are young and energetic, but they often use much of their energies to get through a long work day. The older Asians, on the other hand, may have slowed down substantially in a lot of ways, yet they are fresh in the mornings and ready to be engaged. Older Asian women, as do those of many cultures, often enjoy conversation based on food preparation. You can make great lesson plans from recipes because they require explanations: ingredients, measurements, and procedures. If you have a mixed group with Asians, Mexicans, and other cultures, you can also work with the topic of recipes and discuss differences in foods from country to country. But if you are teaching 20 young fellows who have worked all day and who are primarily interested in getting a step up in their jobs, exchanging recipes would have its limitations. It is doubtful that a group of retired Asians would be interested in spending long sessions on filling out applications and conducting job interviews. But, with a mixed group of students, you can incorporate nearly any topic to a reasonable degree.

Some groups enjoy physical activities, and others just do not want to bounce around the room or do standing song games. What works and what doesn't depend on many factors. The best thing you can do is try to put yourself in the place of your student. If you are teaching evening sessions, you will learn quickly whether or not most of your students are working during the day. You will also notice if they seem physically or mentally tired. Sometimes you will want to use techniques that allow them to relax, yet are not boring. Think how you would feel if you had worked manual labor all day, then you came to sit in a classroom where the instructor did repetitious rote memory work that didn't relate to your particular daily conversational needs. *Snooze!* Sure, you would tend to doze off. On the other hand, consider how you would feel if you attended class for the purpose of passing a college entrance test and the instruction was all based on small talk. The instructor who learns how to teach according to the situation is the one who has happier, more productive students.

Pre-testing and Figuring Out Where to Start

The big question that instructors are faced with from the very beginning is: How do we know how much our students already know? What teachers really want to know is where to start. I wish I had a magic formula for you for this one, but I can offer some practical guidelines for working with an issue that can be problematic under nearly any circumstances. Pre-testing students is tough. I have seen schools go through all sorts of verbal and written tests, but I have never seen a test that consistently revealed the truth about the students' foundations. But do not despair—you can work with the problem if you keep your focus on the students' needs and interests, and on recycling so that you are meeting the needs of more than just a narrow level.

The biggest issue with pre-testing is that of literacy versus verbal skills. While some folks learned to read and write, they did not have the opportunity to practice the spoken language, and many people picked up much of their spoken English without benefit of the reading and writing skills. But the problem becomes even more complex because a good number of the more verbal students do not have a strong base of literacy in their first language, and therefore have no skills to build on.

There are other factors too: Some cultures are not as forward as others, and people who grew up in such a culture tend to hold back. Some students simply will not tell you how much they know—sometimes due to embarrassment or out of their own concern for being slow learners. Often when a student doesn't want to be pushed ahead too quickly, he or she will deliberately not perform well on pre-tests.

Pre-tests as well as post-tests are available from publishers of ESL materials. You will have to find the best test for your situation and for your program, and you might feel you need to modify any test to get a truer reading of your students' foundations. If you are teaching in a medium-sized or large program, there will probably be a committee or group of people who have decided how to pre-test prospective students, and your job will be to work with the students who are sent to your classroom. But if you are the only teacher in your program, then the task will be yours. As you learn more about levels and foundations as discussed in this book, and as you gain more experience, you will come to know what your students need to know in order to handle a particular level. You will also learn how to factor in many of the variables. With all the above concerns, how in the world are you going to get a good feel for how much your students know?

Again, let me remind you not to become discouraged. Teachers have been dealing with this dilemma for a long time; yet they manage to work with the students who are assigned to them in spite of poor testing and misplacements. If a student is terribly misplaced and you have a multi-level program, you will be able to move him or her around. But if not, then you will do what we all do with all teaching problems: the best you can. The good thing is, though, that students will learn if you teach in a way that challenges them to strengthen their foundations, whatever they might be, and to move forward in every session. Every student does not gain the same portion from each lesson, but everyone can learn something. Try looking at the various situations as puzzles rather than as problems, so that your frustration will not flow over into your teaching.

Total Physical Response

Kinesthetic learning is a teaching technique and a learning style wherein a learner gains knowledge and skills by doing something or using something, rather than by sitting still and listening to a teacher or by simply watching a demonstration. In the previous unit, we touched on the subject of the *mind and movement*. Total Physical Response (TPR) is a technique of incorporating movement into your lesson.

You will find that the activity of physical response adds much to your sessions, and even more when it includes interactivity of students to students. When you ask a student to do something *(Please close the door.)* you will observe his or her response and know whether or not the command was understood; that is rather basic. But consider how much TPR you could use throughout a lesson. If the goal is to acquire certain sentence structure or to learn specific vocabulary, you can put the structure into conversation so that they require the learner to do something. *May I borrow your pencil, please?* The student says yes and proceeds to take a pencil to you. *How many tables are there in this classroom?* Someone must respond by counting the tables, then giving you the answer to your question. The action reinforces the memory. If John brings you the pencil, he is telling you that he understands that you want to use his pencil. Once the word *borrow* is made clear, John will associate the word with the action he took in order to fulfill your request. He will learn that word *borrow* implies that the pencil is to be returned. Though it may not have been the highlight of his day, he will remember getting up and taking the pencil to you and your responding with a positive reply that assured him he had understood you. If Sandra counts the tables in your classroom and tells you that there are eight, she will have reinforced her understanding of the word *count* and the number *eight* (and the numbers *one* through *seven*). It is the action that becomes the reinforcement.

To benefit fully from TPR, you must get all the students involved. If John asks Sandra how many people are wearing blue jeans (or red sweaters), you will see some action. Maybe Sandra cannot see what everyone is wearing when they are seated. She might need to ask all the people who are wearing jeans to stand. Then she can easily count those folks. The entire group becomes involved because everyone is either wearing jeans or not wearing jeans. Sandra now answers John's question and moves the conversation further by asking Lee how many people are not wearing jeans. Lee can answer, then ask someone else how many people are there in the classroom. That student can either count everyone or simply add the numbers of the last two answers together. The activities are endless, and you can plan them into your lessons. But more than that, you can incorporate TPR into nearly everything you do. Keep in mind that the more physical movement you facilitate, the more you can reinforce lessons and the less bored your students will be. (Also, the more you involve the five senses, the more learning is likely to take place.) The only warning I might offer is that you should use TPR when it is in relation to language, and not just as an isolated activity. Take into account that some people are shyer about responding physically. I would avoid physical activity as "busy" work. Use all of your time wisely so that everyone can get the very most out of every minute.

Drills and Repetitions

All this talk about creative conversation, and suddenly the cold harsh word *drill* appears. Don't let it frighten you. Used properly, language drills are great reinforcers, and they involve interactivity, as you are saying words and sentences and the class is repeating.

There are times when repetition is necessary – pronunciation, for one. It is important for students to get in the habit of repeating your words. They should feel free to speak them out just after you have said them. You can foster that interaction by conducting regular pronunciation drills. I generally do a solid fifteen-minute drill near the beginning of every lesson. Fifteen minutes of *repeat after me*. It does two great things: it helps the students warm up their mouths and tongues, and it allows latecomers to slip into the room without concern. Later we will discuss pronunciation more, but let me clarify the purpose of the drills here. Students do not learn good pronunciation all at once; they refine it over many practice sessions. Your job is to articulate the words, separate and isolate the problem sounds, and use other words for comparisons and contrasts. Students catch on to the routine quickly, and they usually make an effort to work at it -- for their benefit.

Repetition is also important in setting sentence structure into students' minds, and you can do it periodically throughout any session. If students hear the correct structure enough times, they will turn to it more readily in free conversation. For example, you might be doing a lesson on conditional sentences: *If it rains tomorrow, I will stay home.* Compile ten or so similar sentences all of the same structure. You can easily do a five- or ten-minute drill to reinforce that structure. I suggest that drills never exceed fifteen minutes and that they are alternated with activities that do not have a similar feeling. Have the students repeat the sentence after you and each time write a change-out word on the board.

If it rains tomorrow, I will stay home.	Change to *snows* and *go sledding*.
If it snows tomorrow, I will go sledding.	Change to *Friday* and *go to Palm Springs*.
If it snows Friday, I will go to Palm Springs.	Change to *does not snow* and *study*.
If it does not snow Friday, I will study.	Change to contraction.
If it doesn't snow Friday, I'll study.	Choose a change-out.

You need not be concerned that the repetition feels a bit elementary. Language learners sense that they need this sort of reinforcement. And you will develop a sense of when enough is enough. The important element is that the students feel comfortable to voice the words and sentences, that they open their mouths and say and feel the sounds, and that you help them to understand that all phases of pronunciation and structure are a process and that you are building a foundation that will serve them well.

Pronunciation

Students pick up much of their pronunciation from their instructors, and they do well when the instructor articulates and speaks in a way that the students can hear clearly. Daily drills in pronunciation will gradually improve your students' pronunciation. Make the most of the time by using words that are troublesome, words with sounds and combinations of sounds that are difficult to hear. Remember that some of your students have not been exposed to some of the sounds in English in their entire lifetimes. They did not have reason or opportunity to develop the muscles in the tongue, mouth, and throat that are specific to those sounds. Try mimicking the sounds of a language that is alien to your ears and you will get a feeling for how difficult it is for some of your students. Those who speak a Latin-based language will not have as much trouble as those coming from other languages, due to the similarities and the large amount of Latin-based words that are in the English language. But there are problem areas for all students of English. The rolling of the *r* is stronger in many languages, so the student must work to get that sound flattened out enough to be understood. The *th* is hard for many, and then they discover that there are two *th* sounds (*then, thin*), so they must work on a technique specific to each sound. Observe how you easily position your tongue when you pronounce *then*. Now change to *thin* and feel how you blow air through your teeth. Show your students who are having trouble with those sounds how you do that, but be slow to work with them carefully and slowly, remembering that it is very hard for them.

Some other major problem areas are the *b* versus the *v* and the *b* versus the *p*. Examine your own pronunciation and observe how you are making the sounds. Break that down for your students who have trouble with those sounds. The *r* sounds and the *l* and *w* are especially troublesome for many Asians. Remember that people coming from a more tonal language can have difficulty forming the lips and tongue for such sounds. It takes time to strengthen those fine muscles. Be patient and continue to use repetition!

Take your students through all the sounds of the letters and combinations of letters, but do so gradually and in the context of words, sentences, and lessons. You can easily find lists of words in texts and you will find yourself making up your own lists as you go along. Let's say you are setting out to teach the vowel sounds in the words *kiss* and *keys* because you've realized that many of your Spanish-speaking students have trouble differentiating between them. Write the words on the board and emphasize the vowel sounds. Show the students how you position your mouth when pronouncing *kiss*, and then move to *keys*. It is rather easy for them while you are focusing on the two words, but soon you will hear people shifting back to the habit of pronouncing a long *ee* sound in *kiss*. You will need to go further to break the habit. Make a list of words that have that short *i* sound, and compare them to the word *kiss*; for example: *kiss, miss, risk, disk, fish*, and so forth. Emphasize the vowel sound and have the students repeat it with you again and again. Then create a list of words with the contrasting sound of long *e*; for example: *keys, me, Rita*, and so forth. Continue to alternate between the two sounds until you feel the students have had enough. Then come back to the drill on another day. Drills are like physical therapy: continuous sessions to build up muscles and reinforce memory.

Models and Change-outs

Since mimicry and repetition are at the heart of conversation practice, then clearly the model conversation is an important tool. Texts are filled with useful models for all levels of language structure and vocabulary learning, but none is more valuable than the model that you create from within the group. An example of a text model might be something like the following:

| A. Do you like my new blouse? |
| B. Yes, it's lovely. |
| A. Thanks. I bought it to match this skirt. |
| B. Oh, it matches perfectly. |

The above model offers some simple sentence structures and perhaps a couple of new vocabulary words. With very little effort you could do some substituting of words such as *blouse* to *shoes* and *skirt* to *purse*. You could easily change-out the descriptive words *perfectly* and *lovely* to whatever might challenge the group. But consider how much more interesting the conversation becomes when it originates from the classroom. Naturally it will take more effort to jump-start the group and to write out the model on the board, but the intrinsic motivation is inherent in the process, and intrinsic motivation will do much to help the students internalize the material. You could begin to create the model by asking a simple question such as *When did you buy your _____?*

Select a student who is fairly responsive and warm up a friendly conversation until you get the sorts of sentences that will make a good model. *That's a nice purse. Did you buy it to go with your shoes?* The students might respond by saying, *No, I didn't.* All you need to do is continue probing. *Did you buy it because it is the same color as your shoes?* Don't be surprised that the conversation seems to go awry. That's natural, because people just don't talk in "model" conversations. But you will be able to pick the model out of the natural conversation with that one student or with another whom you pull into the discussion. *Does John's tie match his shirt?* That's likely to lead you into a bit of comedy with the reply of, *No. John isn't wearing a tie.* You will want to tread carefully on personal attire so that no one gets insulted over mismatched clothing (or someone's opinion of coordination and mismatch). You offer a red sweater to someone who is wearing orange and invoke a response such as, *No thank you. It doesn't look good with my dress.*

Now let's put the model together from the above discussion:

A. *It's a little cool in here.*
B. *Would you like to borrow my sweater?*
A. *No, thanks. It doesn't go with my blouse.*
B. *Oh, you're right. It looks terrible. Try my jacket. It goes with everything.*

Next, select some words and phrases for change-outs.

A. *It's _____ in here. (cold)*
B. *Would you like to borrow my _____? (coat)*
A. *No thanks. It doesn't _____. (fit)*
B. *Oh, you're right. It looks _____. (too small) Try my jacket.*
_____ (It's a lot bigger.)

Consider all the possibilities for creating practice with the above model. You could continue on to change out verbs (*borrow/use, looks/seem/feels, try/slip on/put on*); you could add in expressions (*Boy, it sure is cold in here. My, it certainly is. . . . It looks awful. It clashes*). Look at all the new vocabulary you could introduce. The only problem with this sort of activity is deciding when to stop. You do not want to overload the students with too many new issues and words at once. But you will have fun adding in words and phrases that the students offer, as well as the ones you suggest. The definitions are made easy by the change-outs. Though it might be difficult to explain the word *clash* under any other circumstances, in the context of the above conversations, the students will easily slide into the meaning of *clash* from *doesn't go with, looks terrible*. You now have the perfect opportunity to build more vocabulary by adding in more synonyms (words that mean the same) such as: match, *go together, coordinate,* and so forth.

Conversation models can be used at any level, even survival level. For example:

A. Hello. My name is Sarah. What is your name?
B. I am Ion.
A. Where are you from, Ion?
B. I am from Romania.

Models are used continuously in the beginning and intermediate levels, because that is where the bulk of language structure and vocabulary is presented. And, there is a place for model conversation on the highest of levels; for example:

Diego: I am beginning to think that if I had gone to college just out of high school, I would not have gotten as much out of my learning experience.
Sam: Yes, I'm sure you are right. I held off on attending graduate school so that I could learn the ropes of my profession first.
Diego: Do you now plan to go further with school?
Sam: I'm still considering it. There are, however, so many other things in life in addition to study. Tell me, what do you anticipate for your professional and academic future?

Look closely at the sentence structure above and all the challenging vocabulary and language strategy (ways of inquiring in polite conversation). The teacher/student-originated models will become your best tool, so you will want to begin honing the techniques for creating them as soon as possible. The important elements are to engage the students in conversation up to their limits, or the limits of the core group, then add in additional challenges. Select the model from the general conversation carefully so that you have something to build on. Allow the group to offer words, phrases, and sentences and to interact with you and the group, but maintain control of the conversation enough so that you can move forward to build the model, then to work in the change-outs.

Consider your topics and try to work in models that give you the opportunity to pull in the important issues of each topic. For example, if your topic is housing, then you want to be sure to cover the most pertinent aspect of housing for the particular level. That might take a half dozen or so sessions with model conversations. When you suddenly find yourself becoming brain-dead for ideas, it is time to turn to the text. It is not a sin to use the text models; just keep in mind that the ultimate goal is to move the students into free conversation, which comes solely from intrinsic motivation; therefore, it is good to start them out with the teacher/student-originated models. Doing so helps them to get into and remain in the groove of natural conversation.

Present it, practice it, and then perform! Don't forget to applaud it!

Presentation, Practice, and Performance

When you are working with a group of any number, you have the immediate concern of how to break up the session into activities. Once you are sold on the importance of interactivity, you will do everything possible to incorporate it into all sessions. A simple way to do that is to think in terms of three parts: a presentation of the material, a practice segment, and then a time in which the student can perform and reveal their skills. Presentation, practice, and performance (PPP) is a great way for a new instructor to begin, and it will often be the technique to which an experienced teacher returns.

The presentation part is where you will work the lesson. If you are teaching a lesson in purchasing fruits and vegetables at the market, first you will need to identify the items (bananas, grapes, watermelon, lemons, oranges, broccoli, and so forth), then create a conversation with the group; for example:

A. *How much are the bananas?*
B. *They are 50 cents a pound.*
A. *How much is a watermelon?*
B. *Watermelons are $5 each.*

Presenting such a lesson seems easy, but you must spend time with word meanings, pronunciations, and sentence structures. Work it from the model conversation that you have created with your students, and then begin changing out words such as *bananas* to *broccoli* and *watermelon* to *oranges*. If this is relatively easy for the group, you can build on it easily by changing out other key words such as *how much* to *where*. That will take you into the realm of locations and directions.

A. Where are the bananas?
B. They are in the produce department.
A. Where is that?
B. Produce is on the far right side of the store—over there.

When the group has a fairly good grasp of the words and sentences, and most students can remember the model conversation well enough, it is time to break into practice groups. If you have a sizable class, you can easily divide into groups of three. You could allow them to work as practice partners in groups of two, but you will find the groups of three usually become more active. One person takes the role of A and the next person the role of B. Then, the B person changes to A and converses with the third person, who now becomes B. Teach the students to continue rotating the conversation until they've exhausted it. Teach them how to change out words and eventually move into free conversation as their skills permit.

Finally your students will be ready to show off a bit. This is the performance segment. Bring the larger group back together and foster a conversational atmosphere. First, ask for volunteers and have one student start a conversation with another using the model. Just as they learned to rotate A to B from one student to another to another in the three-person group, they can now rotate from the first two students to another. It goes like this: One person asks another *How much are the bananas?* He or she selects someone to answer. The one who answers will proceed to select someone else for a new question. Then encourage the group to use change-out words and to move away from the model. Encourage them to use other words and phrases that they've learned from previous lessons. It might go something like this:

| A. *Excuse me, where are the canned fruits?* |
| A. *They are two aisles over from the produce department.* |
| A. *Thanks.* |
| B. *You are welcome.* |

Incorporating and Ignoring Grammar

It may be that you've already been teaching or will start right out teaching from a text that someone has suggested or handed to you. Maybe that text is totally grammar-based. Or, possibly, you will have access to a variety of texts and you can select the ones that seem the most active, but you will have a concern about teaching grammar. In fact, the issue of grammar is probably the culprit that scares potential teachers away. So, let's begin by putting it in its place.

Grammar: the almighty, master of all languages, bowing to no one. Grammar: the mark of intelligence and proficiency. Okay, now we've gone too far. Exactly what is grammar? It is not the ultimate blueprint of our language; it is simply the observable and recordable patterns of the basic workings of the language at a particular time in the language's evolution. It is the patterns of how words and their components work to make sentences, and the study of structural relationships of language. If an individual speaks English, it can be assumed that he or she also somehow learned the structure, either intuitively or superficially. But the question always arises (and it should): *Does the instructor know his or her subject well enough to teach it?* In the first unit of this guide, you will find a section entitled Knowing Your Subject (page 23). Read or reread that section as you go into the following material concerning the teaching of grammar. Now is not the time to allow it to frighten you.

Again, consider your first language: How did you learn its structure? You simply learned to use the language; you discovered how it works and you became aware, at some point, that some usage is thought to be higher than other usage. *Ain't that so?* And as you went through the years of schooling, from the time you began to acquire pre-reading skills until the time you finished school, you learned the names of the parts of speech and terms that identified the mechanics of the language. Or, you did not fully learn that sort of vocabulary at all, and grammar is a scary subject even today. That is not at all uncommon. I would say that the average ESL instructor learned much of his or her grammar by teaching it. Because we can speak the language, we have enough confidence to take a shot at teaching; then as we realize that we are a bit deficient in grammar terminology, we also find that it is right in front of us -- in the textbooks. We can absorb it a little at a time as we prepare for upcoming lessons.

Most teachers have had the experience of standing before the class, and in the flurry of an explanation of some structure, realizing that we do not know why it is the way it is. We stare blankly out at the students and pray for mercy. Then another question arises -- one that we can answer -- and we continue teaching, nearly forgetting the awkward moment. Later that day, we are frantically searching through books for the answer so that such embarrassment will never raise its ugly head again. And the students? What did they think? Probably nothing at all, because their focus is on learning what you are offering them, and not on catching you in little insecure moments. The pace of the ESL classroom can be so fast that usually something else comes up before you can fall into any terribly deep holes.

Do we need to go through that scenario mentioned above? Yes we do, if we are thrown into a situation as most ESL teachers are. If you intend to teach an advanced-level course, you surely need to be ahead of the game, and you'll get there by studying advanced-level texts. If you are teaching survival-level, you simply need to be aware of what it takes to lay the foundation. But no matter what level you are teaching, you will feel better once you've attained a level of confidence in your knowledge of the subject; then you can put your energies where they belong: into your teaching.

Now that we've dispelled some of the fears and you are still reading, we can go on to the issue of how to incorporate grammar into your teaching. The key, as with most issues, is balance. Surely the elements of grammar will come up as you teach the language, because they are the elements of the language's structure. We cannot avoid them. We needn't avoid them. But we needn't bow down to them, fear them, or put them on a pedestal. We just treat them for what they are: mechanics that have evolved out of the way in which we as humans use language. They were not superimposed on the language by some committee of grammar experts; they were derived from necessity. A noun is a noun because it's a name. A modifier is such because it alters (modifies) the meaning of a word. Conjunctions are so named because they conjoin.

If you are fortunate enough to have access to the better texts, you will come on to each of the elements of grammar in the appropriate time as the issues come up. That, in my opinion, is how you teach grammar -- as an integral part of communicative English. The only exception would be if a student needed to pass a grammar test of some sort, usually for entrance into a program or as part of the TOFEL, the exam that often acts as an entrance test for speakers of other languages into American schools of higher learning. You will find that many students come into your classroom with a strong foundation in English grammar. They love grammar and grammar books because they have been their crutch for years of *explicit grammar instruction*. The problem is they cannot use the language well in oral communication, and often the intended meaning gets lost in written communication. You might feel a desire to snatch their books from them, but don't act impulsively. Concentrate on working with those students from an oral approach. They will soon loosen their grip on the grammar text. Let them know that their past study of grammar has merit and it has provided them with a strong foundation, but now they are in the speaking phase.

If you are working with a full program and you have a comprehensive series of texts, you should be able to lay out a strong underpinning in the mechanics of language structure without ever actually teaching grammar as a separate topic. Avoid discussions that demonize the explicit instruction of grammar, but help your students understand that your teaching also fosters acquisition of grammar through an implicit route, and it encompasses the complete language, with emphasis on the communication essential for their lives, current and future.

Teacher-to-students and Student-to-student Interactivity

Interactivity is the dynamism that keeps the learning sessions moving and vibrant. Learn to use the energy of the students and conserve your own energy for when it is most in demand. When you are demonstrating a lesson (doing presentation) you will need to project yourself fully. Some teachers are much more demonstrative than others by nature, but even the most sedate of us can "feel the burn" after an active and lengthy teacher-to-students session. Often we enjoy that time so much that we forget to shut up (excuse me for being so brash). We continue on and on until we just happen to notice that the group is fading. All we can do now is stop, stand there, and experience the exhaustion from every angle. Not to fear, though. All you need to do is limit your activities to reasonable blocks of time. A twenty-to-eighty percent ratio of teacher-presentation-to-student participation is common, and may be a reasonable goal for communicative language teacher. (This will vary according to the needs of the students, as in the case of students who must prepare for a written exam.) The teacher-to-students session probably should not be more than a half hour, and it should be quickly followed up by an active students-to-students small-group practice session.

During the teacher-to-students session, you will find that you can evoke responses from your students. They needn't feel that they must sit quietly while you explain a portion of material; they can interact with you by repeating words and sentences after you and by answering questions that you bring up. You can involve students totally by creating conversations with them—conversations that require responses. To reinforce the conversation models, you can focus on students one at a time. Create a conversation with an individual who won't be intimidated terribly. Then single out another person. This sort of teacher-to-student interaction helps the others, especially the more timid ones, see that it's okay to speak out and it is perfectly all right to make mistakes. It is all part of the process.

Once the presentation is over and the students are ready to practice, divide the number of students by three and count off. If you have 21 students, you will count off to seven, thereby creating seven groups. If there are 22, the extra person will count off as number one to create one group of four. Move the groups as far away from one another as possible and allow them 20 to 30 minutes to practice from the material you gave in the demonstration. That student-to-student interaction is a great reinforcement. Be sure that they have enough material to stay busy. Move around from group to group and become involved in their conversations. Encourage them to move into free conversation once they've worked over the lesson material. That will become a concern when a group is made up of folks from the same first language, so you will want to encourage them to stay in the English language.

Student-to-student (or students) interaction is effective in the performance stage. After the groups have had time to practice, bring the entire class back together. Encourage a volunteer to select someone else to interact in the lesson model conversation. Then have the selected person choose the next person to interact. Your job now is to be there. Avoid taking over the performance session by correcting a student, and then going into a long explanation or continuance of the original lesson. Just allow the time to be performance, as rough as it might seem. Assure the class that you will return to the lesson later for review. Keep reminding your students that it is all part of the process. That is a difficult concept to teach to beginning students, but you'll find ways to express it. Remind them that "we are not finished." Use that line or some variation of it to encourage folks to return to class regularly.

Games and Other Silly Things

With such stress on activity and interactivity, it would seem that a class session might be all fun and games. And it is great if it feels just that way. Games offer incentives; therefore, they can be of use. They are good for a change of pace, too, but I suggest you use them strategically. The problem is that games selected at random do not usually fit into the course of material that your students probably need to be working on. If you are particularly creative, you can figure out ways to alter games to fit the material.

Bingo can be fun for some groups. When people are studying together frequently, you really need to vary the activities and throw in surprises such as a bingo game occasionally. It is perfect for practicing numbers, and there are inventive ways to change the game to center on identification of items. You could create a vegetable bingo card, then draw a picture of the vegetable from a bowl. Whoever fills his or her card first wins an apple or orange or some other token item. The point is that the students become interested in accomplishment—the filling of the card—and the process acts as a reinforcement for their vocabulary of vegetables, or whatever you choose.

Physical games can be enjoyable too. Do you recall the old game of dodge ball, where the ball is thrown at the individuals in the center until someone is hit? That person then is deemed "out." Rather than using a ball and putting people out, try using a soft item, stuffed with material that represents vocabulary words. Toy vegetables and fruits are easy to use for games. The goal would be to toss the soft stuffed apple to someone around the table. That person must then identify the item. Someone else tosses a pear, and someone else a banana, or whatever you are working with.

The above game would be fun for a very short time and you might use it as a diversion, but again heed the warning that an overuse of games will do nothing but waste your students' precious time. Use games to break the monotony of the usual techniques. Be creative and figure out how to invent a game that truly adds to the study, and if a game does not add value, don't use it. Avoid using any game or activity that might humiliate any of your students. Some adults will participate easily in safe games; however, some folks feel even more alienated when they do not enjoy the activity or they do not understand how to play. The effectiveness of games often depends upon the personality of the teacher and his or her ability to pull off the activity.

Books of games and activities are available to you, particularly those geared to younger children. Make the most of what you can find and add a little light-heartedness to the serious business of teaching language.

Student-originated Teaching Tools

Your students often become a good source of materials. They will bring in game ideas, music, and art items. Often they ask if they can share techniques and material that they have found helpful. Encourage them to do so. Allow your students to do as much of the planning as possible, especially as they move into higher levels. For example: you might be planning a conversation session for the last segment of the day. Have your students write down questions they would like to include in that exercise. You can screen the questions yourself and select the ten best, or you can make a teaching session from the selection process by writing several of the questions on the board and having the class examine them for accuracy and open-endedness.

The following are typical samples:

Where you go after school?
Correction: *Where are you going after school?*
What you do if you was president?
Correction: *What would you do if you were president?*

Even though you have interceded to correct little problems, the questions are still student-originated. That adds a dimension to the conversation session. You know that by glancing at the expression on a student's face every time his or her question is used by another student. Your students can do a lot to add to the class instruction. While it's true that you need to drive the course, you can teach people to steer the activities. Encourage their input and allow them space and time to try things. The only danger here is that you might allow an activity to take you too far from the material that needs to be covered. But if you think in terms of using student-originated tools as *enrichment*, you'll be on fairly safe ground. The students will feel as though they are a strong part of the course of study. You can guard against any one student dominating by involving as many as will participate.

Instructor-made and Store-bought Materials

Once you have developed a degree of communication with your students, no matter how limited their English, you will know something of what motivates and interests them. It will be natural for you to bring items into the class to teach topics in ways that appeal to them. Before you know it, you will be spending time constructing teaching tools, particularly visuals for vocabulary. Of course, if you have or your program has endless resources, you can pick and choose from those, but chances are you will gradually become an expert of sorts at making tools and putting together teaching materials. That will be a great creative exercise for you, because one never knows when he or she will be pulled into a new situation, new level, or new group of people, where materials are not easily available.

Be careful to select pictures from magazines and charts that are easy to identify and easy to see from a reasonable distance. Also, you might consider the content of such visuals to see that they are appropriate to the folks you are teaching. To make an exaggerated point, let me tell you that there was a time in California when all I had was an old (early 1960s) series of texts that depicted all characters as Caucasians with British-American or German-American sounding names. It was embarrassing for me that it seemed I was promoting the concept of making everyone conform to a core group of Americans. My class members were of all nationalities and races, and even though it was still early in the '80s, we were far beyond that sort of image manufacturing. What a relief it was when our school finally was able to afford texts that more truly reflected the people and culture of the area. Try out your instructor-made tools first, but be prepared to abandon them in an instant if it turns out that they do not work for your students. Because your classroom time is always so limited in the first place, you don't want to spend precious minutes fumbling with materials that don't get the job done.

Do everything possible to get access to the great selection of materials and tools that are available through teaching supply houses. Ask in your favorite bookstore, and someone will likely guide you to the large publishers of such ESL materials. Try to make contact with regional representatives of publishers, and ask them for desk copies of a variety of texts. Visit any other programs in your area to see what texts the instructor finds most helpful. Remember always to consider the type of approach you are taking and find texts that will complement it. For example, if you are dedicated to a conversational approach, maybe even a conversation-guided grammar approach, you will not be very happy with texts that are filled with only grammar exercises. Look for texts in which the grammar approach evolves from conversational exercises, and you will be much more comfortable bringing those to your students. Times change, and so do materials. You will feel more on top of the situation if you occasionally re-evaluate all of your techniques and materials. Always be on the look-out for new texts with more innovative approaches to materials. Texts come and go, but the skills and techniques from the better books live on.

Levels and Topics

The nice thing about having an entire series of a great text is that you will have all the topics -- or nearly all of them -- plus all the issues of language structure at your fingertips. Even if the students do not have access to their own copies of the text, you can still use the series to plan out lessons and curricula. In Unit Two we went through an introductory discussion of topics and how they need to be recycled continuously in order to fully teach them in their natural layers. As your students move through levels of the language and acquire a base upon which to build, they will soon be hungry for more in-depth workings of the same old topics. Let's take another look at life topics in relation to levels.

Survival level, often referred to as zero level, assumes that the students have no English. They can recognize words by sound or in writing, but they cannot communicate with those words. This level can be most relevant if the instructor works with identification of words that students need to get started with each of the life topics.

Survival-level students are truly struggling to survive in a new community; hence, they need the very basics: brief questions and answers related to introductions; the names of items in and around the school as well as the names and titles of the people associated with the school; the names of foods and how we use singular and plural with those names; basic vocabulary for work, including the names of occupations and people in the various fields and the names of tools and equipment; the names of body parts and ailments as they relate to health, and the basics of dealing with emergency health and hazard situations; the terms and phrases for buying clothing and other necessities; the vocabulary words related to banking and paying bills, which of course include number and currency; terms that have to do with games, social events, and entertainment and recreation facilities; words and phrases related to individual and consumer rights and individual and community responsibilities; basic vocabulary for expressing opinions; and the skills for tackling language strategies. Can you imagine how many lessons might be involved in the above topics just on the survival level?

Remember always that you first need to lay the foundation. Students will urge you into in-depth subjects, but they soon run out of words and skills. Your job is to keep things on track. One student may come to class excited to discuss all the ramifications of consumer rights, and you will be anxious to oblige so that your student can immediately deal with some sort of consumer problem. That issue will make a great topic for a lesson, but keep in mind that the rest of the class can be easily left in the lurch when the discussion goes far over their heads, or shall we say, their words. *Satisfaction guaranteed?* What exactly does that mean in the American economy and what are the legal recourses available to consumers if they are not satisfied with a product or service? It is a great topic for more advanced levels, or perhaps for an after-class discussion with the students who are most interested.

In addition to the vocabulary to be taught at the survival level as mentioned above, there is more: colors, directional and location terms, time, days, months, time spans, family relationships, and so forth. You will have plenty to work with without getting the class bogged down with more advanced levels of the topics. Continue to reinforce the fact that language acquisition is a process and that you intend to continuously recycle all topics. Always remind your students that they are not finished with a particular topic and that you will come back to it. At the survival level you will need to familiarize the students with the verb *to be* and its tenses, and that is because simple identification requires a term of existence.

The verb *to be*:

This is a book.
These are books.
We are in the U. S.
You were in Mexico last year.

The verbs *is* and *are* simply state that something exists. It is essential that speakers get the usage of the verb *to be* memorizes so that they can build on that basic structure. Survival level is also the time to get students warmed up to pronunciation drills. Again, let me suggest that you keep such drills to 15 minutes or less. Practice simple sentence structures and change out verbs and verb tenses.

Simple sentences:

Every day I go to work.
Yesterday I went to work.
Tomorrow I will go to work.
Tomorrow I'm going to work.

The best tools for this level are visuals! Recycle life topics using the techniques of intrinsic motivation, interactivity, and all the components of language. Beginning Level assumes that the students now have the foundation as described above. Of course, there is still that gray area of *assessments*—some may not have the entire foundation, and some may have much more than that. When students have basic vocabulary, they can use words to build sentences and learn the basics of sentence structure and grammar. The beginning level should build on the survival skills the students bring to the class, and much time should be spent in repetition of pronunciation and sentence patterns. Much of conversation is from models learned through rote memory. As the course progresses, you will notice that a new student-misplacement problem has emerged because of the various levels of oral ability versus literacy skills. Some students seem to be rather advanced, yet they cannot perform simple tasks in writing. They can easily dominate a classroom discussion because of their oral skills, while the others tend to rely more on the written assignments. It is important to find a balance between oral and written practice so that both groups will move forward.

If you have a large enough program or class, you might find it helpful to split the beginning level into two courses, a Beginning I and Beginning II. Many of the students will still need more beginning-level work, but some are now able to create conversations on their own, and that latter group will do well in an advanced level of a beginning course; hence, Advanced Beginning.

Through the beginning levels the goal is to continue recycling the life topics and go into more in-depth subjects within each topic. Visuals are still essential, as are repetition through sentence structures, and pronunciation drills. Create and present conversation models, practice those conversations in small groups, then allow the students to demonstrate their skills. As you work with conversation models, teach the students to change out words and build toward more free conversation. Several of the text series offer many model conversations and substitutions that will take a student through the bulk of language structure. Also, employ good old tried-and-true question-and-answer sessions. Begin with instructor questions, and then move as quickly as possible to student-originated questions (with instructor corrections).

Look again at each of the life topics:

introductions	*school*	*family and friends*
people and places	*directions around the area*	*sharing news and information*
housing	*food*	*work*
health and emergencies	*shopping*	*personal finances*
recreation	*rights and responsibilities*	*opinions*
health and emergencies	*shopping*	*personal finances*
language strategies		

Consider how much material you can glean from recycling the topics as you presented them at the survival level. Once the students have had time to absorb the survival-level foundation, they will be very ready to move on. Don't feel that you must confine lessons to one topic at a time. Allow them to overlap as they may. For example: If you have been using the topic of work and occupations, you may notice a natural segue into the subject of rights and responsibilities. It is difficult to discuss shopping without its overlapping into personal finances. The goal is to facilitate whole language in the most natural ways possible through intrinsic motivation and interactivity.

An Intermediate Level provides time to solidify grammar and sentence structure. The students usually now have enough vocabulary and skill of association of concepts that they can handle the more complex structures, such as those with conditional (real and unreal) clauses. The difficulty on this level is that there are numerous sub-levels within a group of intermediate students; therefore, finding the foundation and the students' goals is difficult. It is important to use a variety of activities and techniques to draw in as much participation as possible. A good balance of drills, conversation, and writing is the goal. Create lots of reason to talk about anything and everything. A primary goal for advanced level is to move the students into that 70% range of language. The students are now concerned that they communicate with the fullest of information and concepts. Much practice is needed in student-created conversation, and familiarity with slang and idioms. Continued practice on the part of student as well as instructor reinforcement is important. In multicultural classrooms the social exchange can be quite dynamic. Parameters need to be set to avoid wasting time with cultural clashes.

If students have approximately 70% of the language, they can function quite well in most situations, but they still have the desire to express themselves fully with skills that would put them into the 90% range. (The percentages relate to commonly used English in an English-speaking community.) That constitutes an *Enrichment Level*. Such a study must come entirely from the students' needs and interests, because only they know what sorts of problems they run into. Idioms should be included, as well as the multitude of expressions used in American English or in the English-speaking community at large (depending upon where you find yourself teaching). An enrichment course could continue for years so that people can attend as they find time, and it can provide a safe place for people to grapple with the finer points of language strategies and offer them the much-needed camaraderie. Levels are certainly no more than arbitrary divisions, and they vary from program to program. They also change within a program as that program grows. It seems, though, that the four-level situation (survival, beginning, intermediate, and advanced) tends to evolve in medium-sized programs with more than a hundred or so students. When programs have hundreds more and even thousands of students to work with, more levels can be incorporated, such as *Beginning-beginning (Beginning I)* and *Advanced beginning* (*Beginning II*).

Moving Conversations Forward While Holding Back the Reins

The primary goal of any language course is to engage students in the language, in which case, all your effort will be to encourage and allow people to participate fully. On the other hand, you will feel the pressure to cover the necessities, and you will find that more often than not, the group will tend to try to exhaust one topic before moving on to the next. That seems the natural way to go, but you will never be able to move through the topics if you don't control the class sessions.

There is, however, an effective technique for you to hone. The trick is in helping the students to understand the importance of moving on, even when they haven't gotten everything that they might want from a topic. Let them know that you will be coming back to each topic on a higher level. Help them to understand the concept of recycling so that they won't feel so anxious about not getting it all, all at once. The concept is such that your students probably will not have enough vocabulary for you to explain it in a certain number of words. You can show them daily or weekly, or however works best, that you have a plan to move forward, then to come back and add more layers to their knowledge of the language. Come up with a few sentences that you can pull out whenever you know you need to go on. *"That's an interesting point."* Or, *"That's an interesting question. We'll come back to that when we have more time."* A smile and look of appreciation for the students' participation goes a long way. *"Thank you for bringing that up. We will talk much more about it next week."*

I am sure you get the idea, and you will come up with expressions that are even more effective. It will not take you long to figure out what techniques and tools do not work, and you can get rid of those ineffective ones quickly. The ones that do work will not work in every situation or with every group of people; however, you can always be confident to return to the basic principles of intrinsic motivation and interactivity no matter what tools or techniques you try, and no matter whom you are teaching.

Survival Kit

How joyful you would be, if after finding you have gotten yourself lost in the forest on a cold evening with at least a day-and-night hike back to safety, you just happened onto a backpack containing a box of matches, a sharp knife, a couple of drinks, some beef jerky, and a few chocolate bars. Ah, the necessities for bare survival. Just enough to let you cut a path into a safer spot, light a fire, and dine on carbohydrates until you can regain your strength to find the way out. So a survival kit for a new teacher would be something like that: the necessities to enable you to keep on keeping on.

There is a similar sort of kit to aid you in teaching students who are at the survival level. These are students who have no useful command of English, and they cannot communicate to make their needs known. They truly must have a companion with them to translate in order to survive in an English-speaking situation. This level is also often called *zero level*, meaning that the student has zero English. Sure, there are words and phrases that they may be familiar with: stop signs, Coca-Cola, TV, Elvis. But for the most part, they have no working English. What they need are the basics: identification of fundamental vocabulary words and of the sounds in the language. Once an individual can identify some number of things, he or she can build on that foundation to increase language. Everyone must start somewhere. Identification requires visuals, either pictures of the objects being named (*book, student, pencil, house)* or of things that represent actions (*sit, walk, study, work*) and concepts (*happy, sad, sick, cold*).

Seemingly there is no end to this level, but the goal is simply to build a broad enough vocabulary that the learner can begin to put things together to form sentences and to get a foundation upon which he or she can build language structure. Of course, it begins with the *I am*: the verb *to be. (I am, he is, she is, it is, we are, they are, you are)* and all the variations, including contractions, negatives, and question and answer forms. It starts like this: *Apple. What is this? This is an apple. What is this? It's an apple. What is this? It is an orange. Is it an apple? No, it isn't . . .* and so on. (Move the apple to a location farther away. Now ask! *What is that? That's an apple.* It's still an apple, but over *there* rather than *here.* Within no time at all you'll expand the lessons to plurals: *What are these? They are pencils. What are those? They're books . . .* and so forth.

You can imagine that a survival class could go on forever by simply incorporating more and more identification. But before you know it, you are adding other parts of speech into the basic simple present tense verb "to be" sentence structure: *What is that on the table? It's a Red Delicious apple. How many apples are there? There is one apple on the table and two on the desk. There are three Red Delicious apples.* Now you have moved into numbers and colors, not to mention adjectives. As you work the students through survival material, you might wonder if you should be teaching grammar, and perhaps you will recognize that you *are* teaching grammar. The thought occurs to you, *How could I not be?* You are teaching students to identify nouns, and to put subjects and verbs together, then modifiers, and on and on. Surely you are teaching language structure, though you may not feel a need to drill a class in the names of parts of speech. (And it's good that you don't feel that need.) Yet, there are some groups of students who will expect such grammar classifications to be a strong component of learning English, and that's simply because it was the way in which they began to learn English in their countries. Also, much depends on their academic background and how they've learned other languages, if any. Probably the purest way to teach English is exactly the way you learned your first language, or as close to that as possible. However, the fact that students may like and may expect a grammar approach can interfere with a most natural approach.

> **Do the best you can to answer grammar questions,**
> **but steer away from spending precious time**
> **giving a few people long explanations about grammar**
> **while others sit anxiously waiting to learn to communicate.**

Remember, the goal of Survival Level is that students acquire a base of vocabulary so they can proceed to level one, or Beginning Level. Also, you will need to spend plenty of time with sounds: the pronunciation of the alphabet, the long and short sound of vowels and the combination vowel sounds, consonant and consonant blends, and signals that indicate a variation of sound. Much of that work can be done through repetition of vocabulary words, but a level of refinement can be accomplished by doing mouth, lips, and tongue exercises, especially for those students whose first languages are more tonal.

So, what's in a survival kit?

Pictures, plenty of pictures, visuals of all sorts, maybe cards with the alphabet, cards that designate combination sounds, and objects that are easily portable. Not the kitchen sink to identify appliances, but certainly you can bring in a pack of construction paper (or perhaps crayons) to identify colors, pictures of clothing and food, body parts for medical terminology (my back hurts, my stomach aches), visuals of locations (a house, school, park, library, job places, capitol buildings), and maps of every sort (US cities, all continents and countries, and local areas and specific neighborhoods). Add calendars for months, days, and seasons, and a clock with moveable hands to teach all the variations of telling time (10:15, half past ten, quarter till eleven, etc.). Your survival kits will grow as you continue building your classes.

Let's see—what else would you need? Anything and everything that will aid the students' understanding and help them to avoid translation. In English *cat* is the word for an image of cat, but the student will have a tendency to want to identify the image in his or her own language, and then translate it into English. The visuals, especially with the word written in large print on the back, will help the student to identify the English word with the image, thus aiding him or her in skipping the translation step that often bogs down language learning. Material and resources for survival levels are truly endless, and you can spend all the time needed to bring the learners up to the place where they feel they can move on into much more than identification and sounds. Move them quickly, as quickly as they are willing, and then allow them to back off when the pressure seems too great. Survival can be a comfort level for a period of time. When it begins to lose its challenge, the students will be ready and begging for a step up.

What's at the heart a survival kit? For the teacher it is confidence so you will persevere; concern and polite consideration for students so that they will feel encouraged; articulation so that the students can hear sounds clearly; and repetition so that the words and sounds will stick. Put those things together into interactive lessons that spring from students' needs and interests, push through each session with emphasis on intrinsic motivation, and the students will learn the foundation necessary to move into the next levels.

Contents of the Survival Kit

The Survival Kit contains some very specific things, plus anything and everything you can find that might be useful and that will allow for interactivity.

Clocks   For hands-on teaching you will want a clock made of heavy paper or cardboard, one large enough that everyone in the group can see it, and with moveable hands so that you can easily change the time. It would be great if you had a number of smaller ones that could be passed around.
Calendars   Months, days, seasons, and dates are essential, and the best way for people to learn them is by referring directly to a calendar. Collect all sorts of colorful calendars with lots of space for making notes of holidays and other specific days. Some calendars will have illustrations of celebrations related to certain days, and those will be helpful visuals as you teach.
Maps   It is important that students identify where they are from and where they are now. A world map, a map of the United States, and local maps that can be easily seen from anywhere in the room would be ideal. You can also make up smaller maps that show the surrounding neighborhoods, and make copies to hand out for lessons on giving directions.
People   Use pictures of people to teach all sorts of things such as family relationships (mother, father, children, grandparents, and so forth).

Time Lines

You can easily make a time line on the board by simply drawing a horizontal line and adding a short vertical line somewhere approximately in the middle and marking that place as "now." Such a visual works well for teaching time, as in "today, yesterday, and tomorrow," and for marking years, decades, or centuries; for example, the middle mark would represent this year, and the student would practice sentences with "live": *I live in the US now. Last year I lived in Mexico.* He or she would write the year, and show a time span of the era in which he or she lived in that location. *I lived in Mexico from 1995 to 1999. I had lived in Costa Rica before that.* The time line helps students focus on now, before, and before that, in addition to future times and events. Time lines can be marked off in increments to suit your teaching needs. They work well for helping students understand the conjugation of verbs. Beyond the present, past and future, you can teach past perfect and present perfect rather clearly. *I teach in Georgia now (mark the present): in 1989 I taught in California (mark the year) and I had taught in Florida just before coming to California.* Present, past, past perfect. Now go a step further: *I have been teaching in Georgia for five years.* Show the time span from the first year in Georgia up to the present, and designate *have been teaching* as present perfect continuous because, though it began in the past, it is still going on at least up to the present.

Colors

Construction paper works well for many colors, but of course you will have an assortment of colors among the clothing worn within your classroom, unless you happen to be teaching a group belonging to a religious sect that calls for the all the same color clothing.

Clothing

Surely you could bring in articles of clothing, but there really no need to overload your survival kits that way. Outer garments are easily visible within the group and you can find good visual to cover any other items of clothing. It is a natural step to combine the teaching of colors with clothing.

Body Parts

The obvious approach here would be to bring in good clear visuals of the body so that students can identify and pronounce words that will help them through situations such as medical appointments or the purchase of clothing. (*My back hurts. My daughter has a stomach ache. His feet are wide, so he needs a different size shoe.*)

Foods

You might be able to find clear visuals of food items in magazines or other advertisements, or you can check into education supply stores. Some special promotions within grocery stores offer charts and pictures of food.

Occupations

This includes identification of all sorts of jobs, the job titles, and the activities involved in them.

Important Places and Locations

Visuals that depict government and public service buildings are helpful if you can get them. Of course, any pictures of places, towns, states, countries will help increase the students' vocabulary.

Do not worry about what you don't have in your survival kit; you will continuously add new items. You needn't go out and buy expensive items. Allow yourself to build up a meaningful supply of items gradually as the needs arise. The kit will be much more valuable that way.

Teaching at survival level is great fun because it is so active.
The students are eager and animated at this stage,
and the energy level is high.

Creating Interactive Lessons

In this unit:

- The Importance of Interactivity
- Alternating Techniques
- Keeping the Focus on the Students' and Instructor's Needs
- Opening and Wrapping Up
- Putting It All Together
- Recycling Life Topics
- Comfort Level, Enjoyment, Accomplishments, and Satisfaction
- Lesson Samples and How to Work Them

The Importance of Interactivity

Look at your lesson schedules carefully and consider how you can break the lessons into segments, each with either teacher-to-student or student-to-student activities. Interactivity is essential to language learning, just as activity is essential to holding the student's attention -- or shall we say to work within the attention span. We might go so far as to say attention disorder, or go even a step further and use the dreaded tag of ADD: Attention Deficit Disorder. WHAT? I can hear the people screaming in defense this very moment. Okay, I don't mean it in the clinical sense, but wouldn't you agree that we all have a bit of an attention problem, especially when we are forced into sitting and waiting, or sitting and obeying -- or even worse, just sitting? And how much more nicely the time slides by when you are engaged in activity, and better than that, interactivity.

Back to the ADD issue for just a moment! (I won't hold you there long since I know you get bored easily.) As instructors we deal with attention concerns on a moment-by-moment basis. All learners tend to move into brain lock-down when their attention wanders. This is expected and, in varying degrees, is within the range of normalcy. So, we needn't feel bad about it; rather we learn to work with it and work it into the lesson plans. That's the beauty of interactivity: It is necessary to language acquisition; it is fun, and time moves by beautifully when you're having fun.

Alternating Techniques

A great way to hold students' attention (and yours) is to alternate the activities and vary the techniques as often as is appropriate for the lesson. Of course, when you see clearly that one particular technique is working well, don't drop it for something else just for the sake of change or just because you wrote your lesson schedule in ink. Use various techniques as attention-getting tools. If you are doing a pronunciation drill and you feel the students waning, stop and redirect to another activity before they are certain they are on the verge of dropping off to sleep. They won't easily see that you have redirected them (I won't tell), and they'll just think you're a great teacher because they are enjoying the lessons.

Keeping the Focus on the Students' and the Instructor's Needs

As plan out the interactive segments of a lesson and you begin to wonder what is going you to give it continuity, put the focus on needs: your needs as well as the students' specific needs. It doesn't hurt to verbalize the needs as much as you can. For example, you can state clearly: "We are practicing this conversation so that you can communicate with your supervisor or your children's teachers better." Or, you might say: "This lesson is in preparation for the next lesson. And what you learn today will help you to express your needs when you go to the doctor." Continuously remind people that building language is like building a house. If you don't lay a strong foundation, the foundation will crack, which translates into "broken English." It's amazing how quickly students learn that phrase. They know that it is what they don't want.

Needs create motivation, and they work to keep you and the students in line and on target. There are times when just mentioning the needs or stating the purpose of a lesson will help to draw the learners' attention into what is forthcoming.

Opening and Wrapping Up

No matter how you begin a lesson, be sure you make a clear beginning. Doing so helps the students to realize that they are learning units of information and skills. Of course, the tried-and-true introduction has always been, "Today we are going to learn about . . . ." My standby is, "Let's get started because we have a lot to cover about . . . ." But any one beginning can get boring, so mix it up -- but do make a point of creating that formal beginning. That little bit of structure allows people to start fresh each lesson with some sort of "Okay, now we are ready to focus on English."

The same goes for ending a lesson. Occasionally I've found myself listening to the sound of my own voice cranking out an ending to a lesson, then stopping abruptly after, "Okay, that's enough for today. See you tomorrow!" My students always look at me with eyes wide as though to say, "That's it?" How rude it must feel to them. I have learned to take a moment -- even if we've gone past the stopping time -- simply to say: "Today we began working on . . . and tomorrow we will move into . . . . See you then. Have a good day." Not only does the wrap-up add structure, it helps build anticipation. That ending may appear as empty words on a textbook page, but for students and for instructor it is a signal of protocol: *We're doing something important.*

Remember that learning English, along with the process of taking in a new culture, creates enough disarray in the participants' lives; the least we can do is force a little order into our lessons and interactions. This may seem uncalled-for in our laid-back American society, but remember that most of our students are not yet accustomed to our society, nor are they comfortable in it at this time. As you work with them, you will come to see that they appreciate those little things.

Putting It All Together

Yes, it is a lot about attitude, yet much about techniques and tools. (I have this belief that if you found yourself stranded in the most remote part of the world with nothing but a practical knowledge of English, and an attitude, you could teach the natives the language. It's been done.) So make use of the attitude; in fact, flaunt it through every part of your lessons. Then when you sit down to work up lessons for the following week, you won't be easily misguided. Putting it all together will come easily once you have ingrained the disposition of real teaching: the most meaningful, logical, and effective way so that the participants will actually be facilitated right into language acquisition. If they are talking it, they are learning it. So, now that you have attitude and technique, you are ready to plan out your lessons. Keep in mind at all times: the importance of interactivity, blocking off time and alternating techniques for ADD, keeping the focus on the instructor's and the students' needs, and opening and wrapping up to add to the order. You are ready to put it all together, to sketch out daily lesson plans for the hypothetical fifteen-student or thirty-student class that is meeting from 6 p.m. to 9 p.m. this evening. (See sample lessons below.)

The first thing to do is pencil in your topic. If the group is meeting for the first time, you'll need to spend a little time with introductions, but certainly not the major part of the session. Then you can select an angle of the topic, one that relates to the greatest number of people. Many people come to class in the evening because they are working in the daytime. If you think this is the case, you could consider starting with job-related issues. That first topic could easily be "occupations," and you could begin by identifying job titles: carpenter, waitress, executive, clerk, secretary, truck driver, assembler, mail carrier, and so forth. Be sure to keep your material broad enough so that you are not eliminating some of your participants. New teachers have a tendency to begin teaching for the more demonstrative students, only to find that those outspoken people are often the ones who move on, leaving you with the others whom you've ignored. Consider how you might facilitate activities that will get people talking, or at least trying to talk. And remember that it is "the trying to" that matters. Much is learned in the process of trying.

What can you do that will allow people to ask questions? How can you reinforce learning through TPR? How can you help with pronunciation? How can you help with writing without singling out people who do not write well, or by putting too much attention on those who have excellent writing skills? What can you do to keep things moving? Can you see your lessons in the terms of building blocks?

What do you want the participants to learn in this particular session? Perhaps some reasonable goals would be to identify a list of jobs; to be able to pronounce the occupational titles; ask and answer a question about, and associate an activity with, each job. Because TPR is a great help for reinforcing memory, you might create an activity wherein each person must carry a visual of an occupation to another class member; for example: "Please take a picture of a carpenter to José." José would be asked to carry a different picture to Sharon. For physical activity you might pile up the visuals face down on a desk, then draw a name for a student to walk up and select one. He or she can then choose another class member to identify the visual. *(Kasha, please tell me what job this woman has.)* Activities such as this can be motivating, challenging and fun for a period of time, plus they get a bit more oxygen flowing simply because of the movement. But be careful not to drag things out to the point that it seems childish or that it gets boring. Watch your students for either of those maladies.

Adults are adults no matter the culture or language, and they enjoy a laugh and they hate the humiliation of being asked to do things that make them feel childish. It's particularly important to have regular pronunciation drills. Also, at any time during a session you might take a few moments to focus on pronunciation. Write the words on the board; single out the problem areas; for example: truck driver has three *r*'s. Two come after consonants and one ends a word. Slow down your articulation and show the students clearly, how you are moving from the *t* sound to the *r* sound. Then emphasize the sound of the *dr* blend. And don't forget the *v* in *driver*. It's difficult for many speakers to differentiate between the *v* and the *b* sounds. Demonstrate how your teeth and lips are positioned, and emphasize the vibration coming from the *v*. You needn't waste time explaining the phonological terms or principles behind the pronunciation; just articulate, separate, and isolate sounds and practice.

You can focus on the spelling of words without drawing attention to specific students' literacy problems. Remember that it is not just a matter of pointing out inadequacies that embarrasses people; holding up a student's good work to show others can be crushing to those who are far from that particular level of writing. All that is needed is to write the words that you are using on the board. Write clearly and slowly so that the students can see how the letters are formed. Literacy in language acquisition is a deep subject and requires careful handling. For your current purposes, think of writing as a back-up to speaking. Those who can write will write to reinforce memory; those who cannot write will begin to get a feeling for their own literacy possibilities. It is important to keep things moving so that every learner feels involved at all times.

That's just good teaching style.

Longer waiting periods between activities can be terribly boring and can waste precious classroom time and, even worse, lose students. Back the activities up to one another and practice your segues. It all gets easier and smoother with experience. It helps, also, to think of each activity as a building block, though they are not necessarily in immediate sequence; for example: You may not have time to accomplish much more than the occupation identifications and question and answer associations in the first session, but you will have that to build on in the next session. Once the names of the occupations are somewhat familiar, you can easily construct simple sentences using them.

Back to introductions: I am adamant about not spending huge chunks of time to go over and over introductions *(Hello, how are you? My name is John. What's your name?).* The trick, again, is to use building block segments: Say you start the course off with some rudimentary introductions the first day. Three days later you might build onto that lesson by adding more questions *(How is your family? How many brothers and sisters do you have?* and so forth). Then on another day add on three-party introductions: John introduces one person to another. Next week you can build on that by teaching the sentence structures needed to introduce several people at a time *(I want you to meet three friends of mine. This is . . . .)* Practice the order of introduction according to gender and age.

Don't wear anything out. People learn well when they take information in layers. They do not need to "get it" completely the first time. Those who do not already know that will learn it from you. Always reassure them: "We are not finished with that lesson yet." As you plan lessons, be sure you can see each one in terms of building blocks.

Recycling Life Topics

You will find a list of life topics in the last handout. Which one you begin with should be determined by the atmosphere, the attitudes of students, and your gut-level feeling of which one will give you a level of comfort to allow you time to get used to your teaching style. With job-related issues, you may have an automatic motivation if you are working with people who are looking for jobs or trying to move into better positions. If you discover that all of your students are stay-at-home mothers, then beginning with issues related to the topic of medical attention

might be in order. That topic begins with identifying body parts, and can move all the way to how to request a second opinion or (on an advanced level) to evaluate and compare health insurance policies. The topic of locations and directions can begin with *"Where do you live and what are the cross streets near your home?"* but it can go to real estate questions such as *"Which high school serves this neighborhood?"* or *"Do you have any properties listed on quiet cul-de-sacs."* You teach English by moving people through the topics over and over again until they have as much competence as time allows.

Comfort Level, Enjoyment, Accomplishments, and Satisfaction

When the room is filled with chatter, *then* you know something is happening. (Of course, you might want to do a language check to make sure the chatter is in English.) It is a pleasure to watch people engaged in conversation in a comfortable way. You can see it on their faces, and if you don't see it, I would say it is probably time to move to a different technique, or perhaps take a closer look at the cultural and social dynamics. Whoa there! Do not act too quickly on this count. Sometimes engagement can look like discomfort, and who are we to second-guess cultural, age, or gender conflict? However, if there is an obvious problem, you'll need to tend to it by mixing up the seating arrangement or the groups. Do it unobtrusively so that no one is adversely affected.

Often such conflicts are not intentional, but inherent in certain matches, or mismatches. If you notice that an older student seems to be commandeering a younger one, then you would do well to pull up a chair with them and begin a conversation that levels the field. Occasionally you will notice a discomfort of men with women and vice versa. One poor fellow in the midst of four women can feel brow-beaten, yet one man and two women is simply a conversation. And every situation has its counterpart. A younger woman can feel inferior with several mature men, and yes, it goes on and on. But usually such problems do not crop up in short group sessions. When you mix things up frequently, fewer problems will occur and when they do, they will last less time.

There is great enjoyment in interacting on a social and intellectual level. The energy in your classroom can be awesome. Then, what is it that keeps the lesson going?

Interactivity? Sure, and all those great techniques, and a little bit of magic. But the accomplishment your students feel when they realize they are speaking English, and that people understand what they say, is the true thing that drives them forward. And you have to be ready to move them as they are ready to move forward. So what creates a feeling of satisfaction for you? Again, it is the feeling of accomplishing something, and something far beyond what sells on the stock market: something that makes a difference in another human being's life.

There is great satisfaction in watching achievement take place. Plus, there is the gratification of knowing you've done your best to facilitate the interactivity that was needed to do the job. I hope you get paid well for your work -- you deserve it -- but if you are in a position to teach for free, there's plenty of delight far greater than anything money can buy. As you plan out each session, keep those elements of interactivity and intrinsic motivation at the forefront, and you can hardly fail.

Lesson Samples and How to Work Them

The following is a sample lesson, just to give you a model to work from:

Survival Level (an agenda for a three-hour session)
Life topic: food
Pronunciation drill: Practice specific sounds for about 15 minutes, and then stop with a promise to continue the drill tomorrow. It is the everyday drilling that really improves people's pronunciation. Though you cannot explain that thoroughly to the group, approach each session with that in mind and students will get the message that it is a gradual process. Remember that the key to pronunciation is to separate, isolate, compare, contrast, articulate, and repeat.
Vocabulary: Use words from previous lessons; for example: *meat, vegetables, produce, fruits, beef, pork, beans, tomatoes, milk, cheese, eggs, salad, radishes, apples, oranges*, and so forth. Select specific sounds for concentration, such as the vowel sounds in all the words, and the stress sounds in multi-syllabic words like *vegetable, produce, tomatoes, and radishes*.

Technique: Go through the list of words slowly, saying them and showing visuals that represent each item. Articulate the words, then write them on the board one at a time. Next, separate and isolate the vowels in each of the words; for example: *meat (m-ea-t).* Now create a short list of words that have the long *e* sound and compare them to the target word: *meat, seat, beat, Pete, wheat.* Don't be concerned that the students do not necessarily know the meanings of the comparison words. (This is only a pronunciation drill, and if you approach it as such, your students will soon catch on. Focus on sounds rather than meanings at this point.) Now, contrast the long *e* sound by making a list of words that have the short *e* sound; for example: *met, set, bet, pet, wet.* Articulate the sounds back and forth: *meat/met, seat/set, beat/bet, Pete/pet, wheat/wet.* Show the group how your lips and tongue position themselves to form the sounds. Go through the same process for the words *beef, beans, and cheese.* Then move to another vowel sound such as the short *e* in *eggs.* Spend about five minutes with as many vowel sounds as you can work in.

✓ Separate the syllables of words like *vegetable, produce, tomatoes,* and *radishes,* and pronounce them according to their common accentuation; example: *veg` ta ble* and *pro ` duce.*

Review of previous lesson: Use approximately 15 to 10 minutes to go back over the material that was presented in the last session. Use a combination of repetition and question/answer. Hold up the visuals, say the names of the items and encourage the group to repeat with you. Then, ask simple questions such as: *What is this?* and *How many apples does the man have?*

Presentation of new material: Show the visuals of the foods and the various food categories, then build sentences with questions and answers: *This is an orange. What is this? This is a vegetable. What is this? Is this a fruit? Is this a vegetable? Is this a fruit or vegetable?* Continue building sentence patterns for conversation until the group has enough material with which to practice. Write everything on the board as you go. Encourage imitation and repetition as you pronounce the words and the questions and answers. Create structure to the question and answer routine so that the students become comfortable with it and can carry it on into practice groups. This session should take about 45 minutes.

Practice: Break the larger group into groups of three people each. Do this easily by simply counting off. Instruct the groups to sit in specific areas: group one on one side of the room, group two in the center, three on the other side, four in the back on one side, and so forth. Instruct the groups to continue practicing as you were doing in the presentation. Show them how to involve all group members by having one person question another person, then that second person can question the third, then the third person questions the first. Continue that rotation until the material is practiced thoroughly or until the students begin to show signs of boredom or fatigue. This session should take about 30 minutes. Now that the session has gone a good hour and a half, a break will be in order. Allow people a comfortable 15 minutes. It will take another five minutes for folks to get seated again and settled down for the next segments.

Performance: Go back to the question/answer pattern that you established in the presentation segment so to warm up the students again. Switch from teacher-to-student questions to student-to-student questions. Have someone begin by selecting another student to answer a question. Supply the visuals and have people give the appropriate visual to one another as needed. That creates a bit of TPR (total physical response): *Please give me the picture of the vegetables.* A student now must be able to recognize the visual and take it or pass it to the person asking. Use this segment to provide students with the chance to perform what they've learned. Again, be alert to their involvement and avoid dragging the segment out too long. It should last about 30 minutes, or maybe a bit longer if there is a lot of excitement and interest.

Conversation: Now go back to a teacher-to-student format and ask questions that push the level up a bit more. *Where are the tomatoes? In the produce section. Where do you buy your food? At the supermarket. Do you buy groceries every day? No, only one time every week.* Also, throw in a couple of questions that will give the group a hint of what is in the upcoming lessons; for example: *How much do apples cost per pound?* This segment can take up the remainder of your time. Some of the students will participate and others will listen as you push further. That's fine. Encourage free conversation, but realize that on this survival level the students are very limited. Use those final minutes to answer any stray questions.

Wrap up: End the session with words of encouragement and praise and a promise of more to come tomorrow (or at the next meeting).

The above agenda can be modified (streamlined) to fit nearly any schedule. It can easily take the full three hours. (Though you may designate a 15-minute break, it will take a few more minutes to get people settled down and back into the learning mode again.) That leaves you with 160 minutes. The pronunciation drill takes 15 to 20 minutes, review might last 15 to 20 minutes, the presentation of the new material takes 45 to 50 minutes, and the practice session runs about 30 minutes, so that you can use any remaining time for free conversation. Be sure that your final words before departing are those of encouragement in the form of a wrap-up.

Beginning Level (an agenda for a three-hour session)

Life topic: occupations

Pronunciation drill: Practice specific sounds for about 15 minutes, then stop with a promise to continue the drill tomorrow. It is the everyday drilling that really improves people's pronunciation. Though you cannot thoroughly explain that to the group, approach each session with that in mind and they will get the message that it is a gradual process. Remember that the key to pronunciation is to separate, isolate, compare, contrast, articulate, and repeat.

✓ Create the drill from a list of words from previous lessons. You might use the names of jobs such as teacher, repair-person, salesperson, police officer.

Technique: Go through the list of words, slowly saying them and showing visuals that represent each item. Articulate the words, then write them on the board one at a time. Next, separate and isolate the vowels in each of the words; for example: *teacher t-ea-cher.* Now create a short list of words that have the long *e* sound and compare them to the target word: *teacher, preacher, reach, leach, peach.* Don't be concerned that the students do not fully know the meanings of the comparison words. (This is only a pronunciation drill, and if you approach it as such, your students will soon catch on. Focus on sounds rather than meanings at this point.) Now, contrast the long *e* sound by making a list of words that have the short *e* sound; for example: *tech, peck, wretch, let, pet.* Articulate the sounds back and forth: *teach/tech, reach/wretch, leach/let, peach/pet.* Show the group how your lips and tongue position themselves to form the sound. Go through the same process for the words with other vowel sound, such as *salesperson, repair-person, police office,* and create comparison and contrast drills. Spend about five minutes with as many vowels sounds as you can work in.

✓ Separate the syllables of words such as *police officer, administrator, principal,* and pronounce them according to their common accentuation; example: *ad min` is tra tor, pol ice`*.

Review of previous lesson: Use approximately 15 to 10 minutes to go back over the material that was presented in the last session. Use a combination of repetition and question/answer. Hold up the visuals, say the names of the items and encourage the group to repeat with you. Then, ask simple questions such as *What is the name of this woman's occupation?* and *What does a salesperson do?*

Look closely!

If you look closely at the material below you will find the PPP (presentation, practice, and performance components.) They work well in nearly any situation.

Presentation of new material: Show the visuals of the occupations and the various activities involved in the work, then build sentences with questions and answers: *Is he an administrator? What does he do every day? What job did you have in your country? What kind of work do you do now? What jobs do you like?* Continue building sentence patterns for conversation until the group has enough material with which to practice. Write everything on the board as you go. Encourage imitation and repetition as you pronounce the words and the questions and answers. Create structure to the question-and-answer session so that the students become comfortable with it and can carry it on into practice groups. This session should take about 45 minutes.

Practice: Break the larger group into groups of three people each. You can do this easily by simply counting off. If you have 30 people, count off to ten, then instruct the groups to sit in specific areas: group one on one side of the room, group two in the center, three on the other side, four in the back on one side, and so forth. Instruct the groups to continue the practice as you were doing in the presentation. Show them how to involve all three group members by having one person question another, then that second person question the third, then the third person question the first. Continue that rotation until the material is practiced thoroughly or until the students begin to show signs of boredom or fatigue. This session should take about 30 minutes. Now that the session has gone a good hour and a half, a break will be in order. Allow people a comfortable 15 minutes. It will take another five minutes for folks to get seated again and settled down for the next segments.

Performance: Go back to the question/answer pattern that you established in the presentation segment so as to warm up the students again. Switch from teacher to-student questions to student-to-student questions. Have someone begin by selecting another student to answer a question. Use TPR as much as possible so that the students have a chance to move around a bit. *Please give me the picture of the police officer.* A student now must be able to recognize the visual and take it or pass it to the person asking. Use this segment to provide students with the chance to perform what they've learned. Again, be alert to their involvement and avoid dragging the segment out too long. It should last about 30 minutes, or maybe a bit longer if there is a lot of excitement and interest.

Conversation: Now go back to a teacher-to-student format and ask questions that push the level up a bit more. *What is the police officer doing? Where does she work? Where do you work?* Have people ask one another questions such as *Where does José work? What does he do on his job?* That will require a student to interview another person to find out what he or she does. This segment can take up the remainder of your time. Some of the students will participate and others will listen as you push further. That's fine. Encourage free conversation, but realize that at this beginning level the students are still limited. Use those final minutes to answer any stray questions.

Wrap up: End the session with words of encouragement and praise and a promise of more to come tomorrow (or at the next meeting).

Intermediate and Advanced Levels

When working with more advanced students, you will need to allow for more flexibility in activity time. Use the same basic models as presented above for the survival and beginning levels, but encourage more free conversation. The more advanced beginners and the intermediate level students tend to rely still on the model conversation, but they can move much more quickly to create their own versions. You can continue with regular daily pronunciation drills and you can interrupt any session to work on pronunciation problem areas as they arise. Below is a sample of model conversations from which you can easily build presentation, practice, and performance sessions. It could be used in an intermediate or an advanced level lesson.

Life topic: rules and regulations

A. *Is it okay if I park here?*
B. *You'll get a ticket, because the sign says no parking.*
A. *Maybe I should park somewhere else.*
B. *Good idea.*

Practice the model orally until the group basically has the sentence structure memorized. Then, change out words and phrase: for example: Are you allowed to smoke here? or You'll get into trouble, because the sign says no smoking. Maybe I should smoke outside. . . . and so forth.

Breaking Down Barriers

In this unit:

- Cultural and Perceptual Differences
- Individual Variations
- Literacy Levels
- Emotional and Mental Barriers
- Inter-group Dynamics

Cultural and Perceptual Differences

When an individual steps in front of a classroom of people from cultures and languages other than his or her own, impressions are immediately made on all sides: teacher to students, students to teacher, and student to student. Every person has some sort of perception of everyone else, and perception is a tricky thing. Since your goal is to help people acquire English, your job is to facilitate each session with the least amount of stress and interference. In most instructional situations that would not seem to be such a hurdle. But when you are working with cultural differences, you are bound to find some inherent concerns. You will want to break down as many barriers as you can to eliminate any warped perception, the sort that inhibits a teacher or a learner. The challenge must be approached with understanding, tolerance, and respect.

You might think that focusing on the concept of human compassion is enough to fix anything, yet reality will raise its ugly head in time. Some aspects of any culture are bound to be intrusive or offensive to some other culture. People have different life experiences and they perceive things differently. I recall a fellow from one of my courses who, though he'd already held a master's degree in TESOL and had just a bit of teaching experience, came into my course to get what he referred to as a "fresh look" at the field. In all the time we discussed cultural differences, he never spoke out on the issues until one day when he revealed all. He said that he had trouble with the attitudes of some of his students years ago, and that was why he'd quite teaching. He said, "I just couldn't stomach knowing that *those people* believe in terrorism."

Surely I couldn't dismiss his concern, yet neither could I encourage him to keep it, because it would always be a barrier to his teaching. Just the term "those people" implies that the speaker has lumped a number of individuals together and given them a label that simply cannot fit all. One would have to have a vast understanding of world history even to begin to comprehend the struggles of other countries and the feelings and fears of tyranny on all levels. The people coming to my classes for my instructional services must be respectful to me as their teacher and to the participants as their fellow classmates, and I must be respectful to them no matter what country they come from and no matter what I think of the politics or philosophies of that country. We cannot begin to alter someone's lifetime of experience, but we can help that person and ourselves to take on a broader perspective of life, community, and global issues. As we spend more time trying to understand what is at the root of world problems, we can begin to understand why some folks feel terrorized by bigger powers, much the same way we might feel the threat of what we think of as the revolutionary or radical "loose cannon." Certainly this is a huge and important topic, but not one that can possibly play out in a language classroom.

My hope is always that there will be understanding among the people in my courses, but I will do what has to be done to remove stress and conflict from each session. During the first decade of my teaching there was a huge influx of refugees into the US from what was then known as the Eastern Bloc, those who had grown up under communist regimes. Then, into the next decade, I saw more and more of the younger generation that had lived their formative years in the Eastern Bloc countries during the revolutions and into the reconstruction eras. Some of them were naturally respectful to the other generation who'd felt forced to leave there before the fall of an old political system. Some of the older generation were not always so compassionate to the younger ones whose parents might have called them *traitors*, but we got on anyway.

I recall a handsome young Southeast Asian fellow who came into my classroom not long after the fall of Saigon. He'd been given the opportunity to go on to higher education in his country. When I asked him to introduce himself, he stood and told us that he'd grown up in a large city and that he was not the low class of the peasant folks in my classroom. That day I felt the air thicken in the room, and I knew instinctively that there would be a major conflict with the older folks who had literally crawled out of Southeast Asia years before from cities and village alike. You can be sure that I promptly moved some students around to lessen the chance of confrontation, though the solution to such a situation is not always so easy. Do what you can to understand people's stances on issues, but you might find it best to do that far outside the classroom.

If class a discussion turns into a conflict, you must do what you can to remove the problem, and that usually involves transferring someone to another class. A cop-out? Maybe it seems that way, but remember that *your job is to teach*, and not to change the world or to fix its problems. Put all your energies into teaching the language and into promoting understanding -- you'll be far too busy with that to try to do anything else in the allotted time. When you sense that there is a conflict between students during a free conversation session, simply redirect by interrupting the conversation to do a brief pronunciation drill. By the time everyone has focused on their *r*, *l*, and *w* sounds, it is hard to get back into any philosophical battles. Conflict can arise among people from countries still at war, or within same cultures through generation gaps, political or religious tiffs, or economic differences; however, respect must be maintained in order for students to participate in the learning of language. The conflicts are often over issues that are very old and entrenched in the countries from which your students come.

The best we can do as instructors is to put emphasis on surviving a new language, in a new culture, in a new world. That might seem relatively easy until you find yourself and your advanced students forming sentences for question-and-answer sessions. People have serious issues, and often they are, for the very first time, in a country where they should be able to discuss their issues openly. But your job is to facilitate the acquisition of language and you have precious little time to do that. If time is given to allow one student to air his or her personal or political issues, then it's only fair that you permit every other student to do the same. Fifteen minutes for Ion, fifteen for José, fifteen for Nguyen, fifteen for Arelia, fifteen for Toshi, and wait a minute. . . time truly does fly. When will you find time for the instruction that is needed to lay a foundation for the learners to move on to the next level?

Equal time applies to all, including the instructor. I have seen a good number of teachers take advantage of the captive audience to promote their own beliefs -- religious or political. I cannot say that I have not been tempted to ramble on about my own views from time to time. As soon as I even begin to do so, I realize that I am opening up a discussion that will require for "equal time" allowance. All I have to do is look at the clock and think how time would get away from us.

I have heard this argument time and again. "My students learn so much when they have the freedom to talk about controversial issues. It's the purest form of intrinsic motivation." That may be entirely true for a few. But -- and mind you, this is a big BUT -- your allegiance is to the entire group and the progress of all the students. If you make time for "the few" (those who gain a lot by heated discussion) the rest of the students are paying in the loss of time. The issue is not about "controversy," but about time. And time is all you and your students have together. You'll want to use it wisely. Use issues to provoke thought and conversation, to tap intrinsic motivation, but curb and redirect when the session starts moving toward being dominated by "the few." Select your issues well and teach your students to participate in the selection. That will automatically put the students on your side.

You may concern yourself with the above issues for a while, yet in time you will learn to project an attitude to the class so that they will sense the boundaries. Though you cannot avoid occasional outbreaks, you will find yourself, for the most part, focused on the job of facilitating the learning of English.

Cultural differences can be handled most easily by paying attention to and allowing students to present their own differences: discussing traditional and contemporary customs, clothing and foods of their countries; exchanging recipes (when appropriate); sharing music and art; and having them teach some words and phrases from their languages. It makes for a great cultural exchange. The higher the level, the more your group can do. Explain that cultural exchange is important in America's multicultural society, and teach people how to conduct such exchanges with respect, dignity, and pleasure. Don't be surprised if they, in turn, teach you plenty.

Individual Variations

It is not uncommon to have within the classroom a great number of differences in addition to those of culture, language, age and gender; there are also differences from individual to individual. Let's say, for example, you go to Mexico to teach high school and your class contains all tenth-graders, all the same age within a year, all with basically the same academic preparation. Would they learn at the same rate? Would they learn in the same ways? Of course not! Every individual has his or her own way of taking in and processing material. Some would be more verbal and some would prefer the written word. And it goes far beyond auditory versus visual; it goes to issues of exhibition and inhibition, concentration abilities, personal distractions, and an array of other elements that make up individual variations.

Literacy Levels

The ESL/ESOL classrooms in the US, especially the adult levels, have not only cultural, language, gender, age, and basic individual differences, but literacy differences as well. That makes for a huge spectrum -- and yes, all in the same classroom. The larger your program, the more you will be able to sort out the level differences, but you will still have within your group a wide range of literacy, from zero to proficiency and everything in between.

You needn't go insane over this, though I'm sure a few instructors have. The trick is to do the best you can with what you have. If you can change things, that's great. If not, or until you can, allow yourself and your students the flexibility to work with the differences. I have taught classes that had students ranging from a medical doctor to a woman coming from a language that has no written form. José, who was about 32 years of age, was quite proficient. May, on the other hand, had never written a word in her life until she stepped into my classroom at age 45. Both were a bit shy. The two found one another and began studying together. May was more verbal because she didn't have reading skills to use as a crutch. José was fascinated that someone could learn a language without the benefit of writing; therefore, he gleaned much from her. Surely it wasn't the optimal learning situation for either of them. But under the circumstances, it worked fine, until José moved on up to the next level and May happily remained on safe ground to continue working through the letters of the alphabet.

Emotional and Mental Barriers

Isn't all the above enough? Why dig any deeper -- cultural, language, gender, age, and literacy differences, all in the same classroom? Perhaps now is a good time to go back and review the question, "What in the world are you getting yourself into?" Remember that you are working in the field of language arts, not science. Facilitating language is certainly an art, and you will find yourself gradually becoming a student of human nature, with all its positive and negative characteristics. People who are learning a new language are also usually assimilating or trying to assimilate a new culture, or at least some new cultural twists. Some are just excited and highly motivated, while most are anxious, to say the least, and a few are scared nearly to death.

Isn't it frightening enough to try to function daily in a new land? Imagine that you can never -- or at least not for a very long time -- return to your homeland, and learning English is a matter of pure survival. If you can make the language work, you can get a job or a better job. You can break out of the isolation of the language barrier. You can continue to communicate with your children as they become Americanized (whether you want them to or not). And you can have some sort of communication with your grandchildren -- if you're lucky. Or, you can fail and be thrown into some heap of disgraced others who just couldn't learn. Gosh, what pressure! Not all of your students have that sort of stress, but I would imagine that more do than we are aware of. Others simply feel they have to keep trying even when they are tired or bored, and they sometimes try so hard you think they might explode. And of course, there are those who are afraid to try, and they so easily drop out. What is your role in all of that? Yes, you guessed it. Work with all of those students, and all at the same time. A lot of your work is that of desensitizing people, helping them to relax and understand that acquiring English is a process, and that you are patient, and you're there to help them.

Inter-group Dynamics

With all the differences mentioned above, it might seem that you are sitting on a keg of dynamite rather than readying yourself to conduct nice neat little lessons in language. But somehow life goes on, humanity rises to the occasion, and you are there to facilitate it.

A key to creating good dynamics is to hold a strong but flexible rein on each session. It's just good sense to hold on to the time and do what you need to do to control the direction of the sessions. Use the students' energies, prod them, and sometimes joke and provoke them into conversations. Provide them with parameters so that they are relatively safe in using the language with one another, without insult and injury (or at least it is kept to a minimum). Encourage interaction by dividing the groups differently each time, but then watch for stalemates. When you see that people simply are not communicating, you can intervene and subtly help them get the interchange going. If you feel they just can't interact for some cultural, familial (mother-to-son or perhaps siblings), or individual reason, quietly switch some folks around. If the problem seems to be with one person, move another person rather than calling attention to the troublemaker.

It would be so easy to take advantage of your more helpful students, to place them with the problem students each time, but to do so may be detrimental to the helpful students. Watch that you don't get into ruts or patterns of problem-solving; change your MO (method of operation) each time. Your goal is to break down barriers, watch for new ones that arise from fixing the old ones, and try to keep a comfortable balance in the classroom so that everyone can participate, interact, and learn English.

Setting and Meeting Student and Instructor Goals

In this unit:

- Setting Goals While Focusing on Student Interests
- Going from A to B, but Where Is A and Where Is B?
- Setting Goals for Building a Language Foundation
- Using Arbitrary Goals
- The Extrinsic Becomes Intrinsic

Setting Goals While Focusing on Student Interests

The objectives for each teaching situation may be different, yet the basic principle is the same: move student skills from point A to point B while allowing for variations in individual achievements. That is, without a doubt, the goal. Once you have found the foundation (as best you possibly can) of the group's knowledge and abilities, it is simply a matter of building on what students already know and then moving forward. The foundation will reveal itself more and more as the instructor works with the students; the goal then simply becomes point B.

Not only is the act of setting goals a great help to you, but because you appear to see them clearly, the students get a feeling that they are always moving toward specific objectives, or progress markers. That statement may sound ambiguous, yet look at it closely; or better yet, think back through your own learning experiences and consider how your instructor's attitude influenced yours. I recall that in my freshman grade of high school, Mrs. Hoover desperately wanted us to get hooked on reading classics. When she pushed us through *Treasure Island*, one chapter at a time, even reading it aloud to us, we got a feeling of her goal. And though it wasn't something any of us would have tackled on our own, we somehow knew that there was richness lying just below the surface as she read those engaging lines. Oh yes, she had a goal. It did not matter that it took me 20 years to fully understand that goal, but the fact that she seemed driven to impart something of value made the goal seem all the more desirable. I felt I was moving forward as she read to us, and that was enough for me.

As ninth-graders we did not have enough of a frame of reference to fully appreciate what Mrs. Hoover was doing; it would not have done much good for her to explain it. But your students, assuming they are adults of some maturity, will have a frame of reference (from their life experience). Though their English may be too limited for you to give them full explanations of the immediate objectives and the ultimate goal, they will recognize them as they are revealed. Goals and objectives serve a two-fold purpose: they help keep the instructor on track, and they work to motivate the learner. They are the carrot dangling just out in front so that when a student hits a mountain of frustration, he or she can look straight ahead and focus on that most immediate carrot, or objective, and keep moving toward it while the frustration subsides.

Going from A to B — but Where is A and Where, Pray Tell, Is B?

The students' foundation in English definitely exists, yet it seems terribly elusive to a newer instructor. That, however, needn't be a major point of frustration for you and students unless you allow it to be. The foundation becomes recognizable when you see that most of the students are comfortable starting out with a particular lesson. You are moving them from safe ground into new territory. Though they may have anticipation, they do not show expressions of frustration or boredom. They are interested and ready for the challenge of the upcoming material. Their attitude of anticipation is an indication that you have sensed where the foundation lay, though you may not be able to put it in writing or orally describe it in detail. Now you and your students are moving toward point B with a good degree of confidence. But where is point B? And how in the world can you incorporate it into your lesson plans if you cannot even say what and where it is? True, you cannot always pinpoint the exact goal and the exact moment at which your students will arrive there.

What you can do, however, is learn to think about goals with more flexibility. Say for example, on survival level the goals are quite distinct because the students must build basic vocabulary in order to move into a beginning level. Students need to be able to recognize sounds and to verbalize them enough to be understood; therefore, the goals for the early levels are rather obvious: they must master the rudimentary vocabulary of life topics, along with the simple question-and-answer sentence structures in affirmative and in negative. If you have a specific amount of time, maybe 12 weeks, with four sessions of three hours each per week, it is relatively easy to figure out the time allotments for goals. Divvy up the material and divide by 12, then by four. (You might think you could divide it by 144 hours, by that doesn't allow for breaks, transitions, and delays.)

Next, gauge how much time each portion of material might take. Consider that the students will advance through some material far more quickly than some others, for several reasons. The true "survival" student does not yet have the sound system down and he or she is struggling with mouth, lips, and throat muscles in order to form the sounds. Once those tasks become more comfortable, the student will learn words faster. Some groups will have more familiarity with some material simply because it relates to elements in their own language; for example: numbers or denominations of money. Some students will labor through material for which they have no frame of reference from their culture or language. Of course, those coming from alphabets that have nothing in common with the English alphabet will need more time to meet early goals.

You cannot figure out all of the above when you are coming into the situation as a new instructor, but you needn't let that upset you. It will come in time, and in the meantime you can keep your goals flexible enough to allow for almost anything. When even that is not enough, you can regroup afterward and re-establish your goals accordingly. The students will not always be aware of your exact goals, but they will benefit from the fact that you seem to be moving them toward goals. As they become more verbal and as you become more experienced, you will be able to discuss goals, and the students will even be able to participate in the setting of them.

Setting Goals for a Language Foundation

One solid way of looking at language goals is through the steps of language structure. English contains certain elements that need to be mastered so that the language can be used effectively. Call those elements grammar if you want to, but the term language structure has so much more of an integrated and comprehensive feel. Grammar is simply the ways in which words and their component work within the structure. When teachers get together, the topic of grammar is bound to emerge. "My students hate grammar." "I would never teach grammar." or "All students of language need to be taught grammar, don't you agree?" Or, "Ours is a grammar-based program."

How can we argue with any of those statements? In fact, how can we separate grammar from language? Without the meaningful use of language, grammar is absolutely useless, and feels that way to students who are hungry for meaningful communication. Sure, it can be a mental exercise to conjugate verbs and learn the parts of speech, but dealt with alone the challenge will not last long, and it will simply turn into to a rote memory task. (There are actually times when you will need to rely on rote memory tasks, but they won't fare well as the base of a lesson.) So, teaching grammar is best done as such an integral part of the course that the student can hardly recognize it. Think back once more to your first language. How did you learn grammar? Aha! You learned how to use the language first; then in school years later you took on the study of grammar as an academic subject. That worked just fine. The problem is that a second-language learner generally doesn't have that kind of time. It is essential that he or she learn how to use the English language for communication as soon as possible -- not to shortcut grammar, but to master it as part of that usage. Though the term grammar often gives a lesson or course a hint of dignity, what you are really after is teaching people how words work within the language. That feels like more of a down-to-earth approach. The point is, use whatever terminology gets the job done.

In theory, it sounds terribly difficult to deal with grammar, but it really isn't. The points of grammar are steps in the study of language structure; they are building blocks and a perfect basis for considering goals. A lot of your approach will, and should, depend upon the students' orientation. If you have people who've come from academic studies of language, you'll find that they probably already have a good grasp of grammar, perhaps even beyond your own (especially if you were educated in the US.). But for those students who didn't come from academic situations and who want just to speak and/or read and write the language, there may not be any foundation of grammar, let alone a broad base of language structure. You will need to help them build it. If you separate grammar from usage, the students will feel a tremendous lag in their learning. While your students want to communicate, you will be forcing them to do repetitive grammar exercises. On the other hand, if you integrate grammar into meaningful communication lessons, the students will get what they need as they need it.

But now your concern might be: How can I teach grammar or language structure if I'm not sure I truly understand it? The answer is simple: Learn it! You might want to reread the section entitled "Knowing Your Subject" in Chapter One; then go to Appendix A: "Basic Elements of Language Structure," which will act as a quick reference guide for you. You can work your way through the refresher course there. Refresh your knowledge and understanding of language structure and the terminology of grammar gradually, as you teach it. What you'll find is that you actually do know it, because you've been using the language and its structure for many years. What you may not know is the terminology associated with it. That terminology is available to you in nearly all ESL/ESOL texts. Remember that your job is not to teach grammar terminology, but to teach people how to use the language. Grammar terminology is merely a tool. The terminology is a way of referencing the elements of the language. Learn them and use as needed. Don't get hung up on picky terms or differences in terminology, such as *continuous* tenses versus *progressive* tenses -- the terms mean the same thing. If you are teaching an advanced level, you will probably need to stay a few steps ahead of your students, at least until the terminology becomes familiar, and you may need to relearn some usage. (That could be painful, but it won't hurt you in the long run.) Remember that it is all available to you in texts. What you truly may not know is the sequence of the steps of language structure. Get hold of a good series of textbooks and look at the progression of grammar and sentence patterns. You won't ever be teaching it all at once, so take time to gradually become more familiar with it. Also, take advantage of those steps for setting goals for your lessons and your curriculum.

Using Arbitrary Goals

It is difficult when you are starting out, because you have so many unanswered questions about the students' foundation, and about how to set goals. Sometimes just having an arbitrary set of goals is helpful, though you must be willing to give them up at some point and allow more realistic goals to take their place. Just for the fun of it, let's play with some arbitrary goals for a beginning level. Assume that the class has been through survival level and that they have those necessary rudiments so that they are familiar with the sounds of English and they can verbalize vocabulary basic to life topics, plus they can construct simple question-and-answer sentence structures in negative and affirmative.

Now what is your goal? To take the group from that foundation to the place where they can move on to a second level. It will help to know what the next level might consist of, so let's consider what a second level might be. (Remember that survival is often thought of as zero level, and beginning as level one. Level Two might be an advanced segment of the beginning level, or perhaps referred to as Beginning II -- all depending on your program's size, or the pure lack of program.) Students will need to be able to clearly state personal information such as their name, address, and where they are from, and they need to become comfortable with introductions that use more English than the just the basics. They need to be able to use present continuous easily (*What are you doing? I'm cooking. Are you working? No, I'm not. I'm resting today.*) They need to be comfortable with all the pronoun forms: subject and object and possessive (*I, me, and my*). They need to be able to use negative and affirmation short answers (*Yes, I do. No, he didn't.*). The students need to acquire skills in verb tenses so that they can shift from simple to continuous in present, past, and future fairly smoothly. They should be familiar with prepositions and use most of them accurately (*on, in, under, above, beside, at, next to, around the corner, across from,* and so forth). They should comfortable with numbers, amounts, the change of verbs from singular to plural (*There is one, there are two*), and the countables and non-countables (*orange juice, an orange*). They need to know the adverbs of frequency (*always, usually, sometimes, never,* and so forth). They need more vocabulary, which includes words and expressions of casual conversation feelings, time expressions, and directions. Yes, they need all those elements mentioned above to be ready for the next level. So there is your goal and all its elements.

If you take the above elements and divide them into sessions, you could easily set up arbitrary goals for a beginning class. If you allow yourself the flexibility to work with the various differences in the students' learning rates, you could conduct a course smoothly with the knowledge that everything is negotiable. That is probably the way that students learn the very best. It is later, when the instructor or the program begins to force fixed goals on the classes, that people get slighted and short-changed in the process.

You can set up arbitrary goals for any level by simply referring to several textbooks on that level and using their breakdowns of the material. That's the easy part. The hard part is gauging individual sessions for a specific group of people. Again, remember that the key is flexibility, and flexibility is not to be confused with looseness.

When Extrinsic Becomes Intrinsic

You will soon find yourself thinking about goals in relation to you students' level of motivation. A major daily goal is to keep students working from their inner desire to learn, their intrinsic motivation, where the reward is nothing but their own personal satisfaction in learning. That, naturally, is the magic in teaching, but often they just flat run out of gas. It might be because they've absorbed as much of a particular topic as they have a current drive for. It might simply be that you need to change topic, or maybe activities, or it could be that you need to impose some "good old" extrinsic motivation to sort of jump start the intrinsic motivation. Sometimes we just need to offer some sort of reward. I certainly do not suggest offering monetary rewards or even any material item that is in any way costly. The very best external motivating factor for most students is the instructor's praise and the classmates' admiration for accomplishment. But occasionally you will come across tricks and treats that add just enough to get the students back into the self-starter mode. I once knew a teacher who baked marvelous cookies with M&Ms in them. She would build up such anticipation for winning a cookie that the students would get excited, even if they later gave their cookie to a fellow student. Any kind of little contest can work for a short time, though you'll want to be careful that you don't set up a terribly competitive atmosphere wherein some people regularly lose.

It is often just the excitement that works. The hope is that you won't have to rely on the extrinsic for long before the students again become engaged in learning for learning's sake. The goal of extrinsic motivation is always to get to intrinsic motivation.

Writing Goals into Lesson Plans

Simply considering goals will be helpful in your teaching, but the more practical approach is to write them into lesson plans and into curriculum, to remind yourself of the goals and help others see that your daily teaching and your course planning are done with purpose rather than haphazardly. As you plan out lessons, make a habit of considering what "point B" might be, and use that as a goal. Write it into the lesson and write it in a way that allows for flexibility. Do the same if you are writing course proposals and curricula. Instead of writing that "the students will be able to pronounce all the sounds of the language clearly," write that they will "be able to distinguish the sounds of the language and use them so that they can communicate well." The latter is much broader. The first statement could easily get you into trouble, because you are bound to have some students who might not be able to clearly pronounce all sounds, yet they are able to communicate. Also, keep in mind that if you lock yourself into some impossible written goal, it could be used against you in post-assessment and it could jeopardize your professionalism.

The setting of goals is an important part of lesson and curriculum planning, but you needn't wreck your psyche over it. Think of it as a way to evaluate your progress and your understanding of your students' interests and needs, and of a way of motivating your students to be continuously moving forward. You need not ever be upset over not meeting goals; rather, you can use the situation to regroup and to learn something new about the process.

Developing Custom-Tailored Lesson Plans

In this unit:

- Establishing a Protocol
- Tutoring Situations
- Small Classes
- Single-Culture Groups
- Multicultural Groups
- Teaching Children
- A Multifaceted Approach

Establishing a Protocol

Protocol must seem a peculiar topic with which to begin a unit on lesson plans, as if there are suddenly stringent rules or formalities involved. That is exactly the point: There is no set protocol, and it is entirely up to you to establish some sort of proprieties into your daily teaching. Whether you are planning lessons for the traditional levels or creating custom lessons for special situations and groups, it is still important to maintain a classroom structure. (See Unit Four for the basic issues of creating interactive lessons.)

There are general misconceptions that the instructor can simply stroll in, lean comfortably back against the teacher's desk, and chat with eager learners. Once in a while it actually feels that way. But much more structure is needed if language learners are going to progress and if the teacher is going to survive; and this is something that the instructor must establish. In order to conduct a class and facilitate a group of people within a block of time, you'll do well to plan out some things so that the students truly feel they are in a classroom. Otherwise, the precious time could easily just continue as chat sessions that go off on all sorts of tangents. That might seem fun and appealing for a while, but trust me, it will get old fast -- for the students and for the teacher. Serious students of language need to see where they are going.

It is wise to create lessons with a fairly consistent agenda, with some regular activities that students can count on, and with time periods that work effectively for the particular group of students. Each day that you walk into a classroom or teaching situation, you should have a plan for that chunk of time. Be sure always to allow yourself plenty of time to plan out your lesson and to build in some consistent order so that your students can understand what sort of conduct is to be expected from them and from you. There is so much that they do not know, and simply offering a sort of code of conduct (with all the necessary flexibility) can help them to know how to navigate. A rather standard format for a daily lesson might look like this:

1. Warm-up (pronunciation drill)	
2. Review (of the previous lesson)	
3. Presentation (the new material)	
4. Practice (in small groups)	
5. Performance (large group)	
6. Conversation (open forum)	
7. Wrap up (praise/the mention of material to come)	

A morning session might look like this:

9:00—9:15	Pronunciation (drill for warm-up)
9:15—9:35	Review (of the previous lesson)
9:35—10:30	Presentation (new material)
10:30—10:45	Break
10:45—11:05	Practice (in small groups)
11:05—11:25	Performance (large group)
11:25—11:50	Conversation (open forum)
11:50 —12:00	Wrap up (praise students and advertise next lesson)

Tutoring Situations

In some ways, tutoring can be the easiest of teaching situations, and in other ways it seems the most difficult. The ease comes from the fact that you generally have just one person (or possibly two in some cases) to focus on: only one foundation to figure out, only one set of goals, one set of pronunciation problems, one literacy level, only one individual to interact with. And that single number *one* is the same reason for the difficulty: only one person with whom to create interactivity. That means that at least half of the energy must be generated by you. You must keep the interaction going, at least until the pupil has come up to the level where he or she can initiate conversation. Your daily lesson plans should be made up of activities based on goals set first by you, then by you and the person you're tutoring.

The approach is basically to work from student needs and to use intrinsic motivation (though it will often have to begin with an extrinsic force), incorporate the life topics and angle them so that they begin somewhere near the student's foundation, and so that they are meaningful to that individual. It is easier for a single student to become bored when the topic is not directed at him or her. In a group, that individual can benefit from observing the ways in which other students relate to a topic, even when the angle is not his or hers precisely; however, in a one-to-one tutoring position that rebound is not there. Prepare lessons that vary the activities: Begin with warm-up type drills (pronunciation and intonation), but don't linger there too long. Such work can feel rather repetitive on a one-to-one basis, and quickly becomes tedious and tiresome. Because you are working on an individual level, you can discuss issues that the student brings up. You will, however, want to guard against becoming so personal with the student that it feels uncomfortable. That can create pressure for both of you. Lighten up any conversation that seems to hinge too much on personal issues and opinions.

If you are tutoring someone in their home, you will have lots of visuals all around. Use them. Also, bring in items and visuals as needed to present lessons. There might be a tendency to focus only on issues and items in the home, but you will still have to incorporate them into the bigger picture of language structure. It will be helpful if you can select a text and accompanying workbook for your student to follow, and of course, that will help you to follow its structure to some degree. Remember that even with an individual student, the verbal interaction is the most important technique. Use all materials to help you both get conversations going. Protocol becomes especially important in the one-to-one situation, because you need to keep the sessions under control. You can establish a code of conduct gradually, and that will take pressure off of both you and the student. You won't need to be continuously bringing the learner back to the lesson. He or she will understand and accept, for the most part, that you need to follow the lesson plan. Think in terms of three segments to each session, and don't forget to offer a break midway through. Of course, you cannot create the PPP (presentation, practice, performance) format as clearly when the practice and performance segments will hardly be distinguishable. You can, however, always figure out a way to block off time into segments, even if you have to bring an egg timer to break the segments.

A two-hour tutoring session might look like this:

2:00 - 2:10	Greeting and casual conversation
2:10 - 2:30	Review (of the previous lesson)
3:30 - 3:00	Presentation (new material)
3:00 - 3:05	Break (stand up, stretch, take a short walk around the house)
3:05 - 3:30	Practice, performance, and open conversation
3:50 - 4:00	Wrap up (praise student and advertise next lesson)

Small Classes

A nice tight little group (maybe three to seven people) can be such a delight to work with, but again, you have that inherent problem of generating interaction into your lesson plans. It is just you and the small group. They can learn a lot quickly if you utilize a variety of activities and work in segments to keep things moving. Be sure to mix students so that they don't depend on the same "friend" as a practice partner each session.

Because your group is small, you will have more difficult getting people to depart from the core group's interest. For example, if you have five people in your class and four of them have a lot in common, yet the fifth doesn't, he or she can easily feel just like "a fifth wheel." It is up to you to guide the group into topics and angles that will cover more than just a focus on the core group's interests. You will want to be careful not to create a feeling that every topic must be selected just to suit the fifth individual. Keep the topics broad enough so that everyone can be involved and therefore benefit.

If you have a huge gap of level differences in the small group, it will stand out more than when you have a greater number of people and contrasts. Sometimes it is impossible to use a focused lesson plan with a wide range in a very small group. All you can do is the best you can do, then hope that the folks outside the core group will hang in there until the group become larger and splits into two classes. *Hey, I never said this would all be easy.*

Single-Culture Groups

If you find yourself in a location where everyone, or nearly everyone, is from the same culture, your classroom will reflect that. There are pockets throughout the US where single cultures dominate. Of course, you might go to another country and naturally have a single-culture classroom. In many ways the situation is easier because you don't have to be concerned with entertaining the various interests of diverse cultures, and your students will have the same basic pronunciation issues. Lessons plan can target the group more directly. Be sure to follow through on pronunciation practice. It is inherent in working with people all from the same language that you will hear their accent and pronunciation problems so often that they will at some point seem to sound correct to you. Before you know it you may even pick up their accent to some degree.

It will help you to learn as much as possible about how that single culture is accustomed to learning. For example, if you are teaching a group of all Colombians, you will discover that they are used to approaching language in a particular way and you can incorporate those techniques into your repertoire. Or, if you find that all your students are Japanese and they've all acquired a foundation in English from textbooks but they lack the verbal, you may want to concentrate on a conversational approach. As you discover significant elements about your single culture, you can built lesson plans around those.

Multicultural Groups

The richest variety and in some ways the greatest challenge is the multicultural group. You will not only have the diversity of languages and cultures, but of age and literacy backgrounds. Topics abound; the big concern is of how to angle them so to meet most of the needs and interests of everyone. Be sure to keep subjects broad enough that students can apply their own angles, be sure to plan lessons that will lay a strong foundation, and be certain that you incorporate a variety of techniques and styles of teaching, to offer opportunities for everyone to learn.

In pronunciation drills you will have a variety of sound difficulties to address. Be careful not to linger on the elements of one group's problems areas to the exclusion of the other students. Also, you will notice that students have more trouble understanding one another. Maybe that is a good thing, in that it forces people to speak in a way such that more people can understand them.

Teaching Children

If you are teaching children in the US, you are most likely involved with a public or private school program. Most schools require teacher training that focuses on techniques for teaching young people (kindergarten through grade 12), though there can always be exceptions. Then there are the children in other countries. A country may or may not have English classes within its school system; nonetheless, there is a demand for children to learn the language in many countries. Much of the teaching takes place in schools that specialize in English, and they are often private ventures. They need people who not only teach the language but who also work well with children.

The teacher does not necessarily need to be well-versed in all level of language structure. What he or she needs is skill in facilitating children. What would you imagine to be the biggest concern with teaching children? You probably guessed right. It is the challenge of holding their attention. Some people seem to have a knack for such things, and others struggle with it to the point of frustration. If you are planning to teach in another country and the job offers for teaching children are quite alluring, now is the time to focus on the techniques that could very well save your sanity.

What sort of learning atmosphere works best for what ages of children, and how can that atmosphere be achieved? Begin by looking closely at very young learners, say between kindergarten age and pre-adolescent years. They are in a crucial time of their development, and their education is a big part of their daily activities. Children mature at different rates and they often experience startling spurts of growth and development. We can keep the issue of individual differences in mind as we teach; however, we also learn a lot by focusing on what might be the *average* for children of a certain age in relation to how they learn language.

If the school where you are teaching has developed a fairly comprehensive program, and the children have been attending since they were about five years old, then you can see the levels more clearly. The younger children are truly beginners. In a couple of years they gain a base of vocabulary, but they are still in the beginning stages. They can, for practical purposes, be seen as beginners and advanced beginners. By the time they are pre-adolescent, they might have a substantial base in language structure so that they could then move into a more intermediate level. (These discussions are based on arbitrary levels, and levels vary in relation to teaching techniques and tools and to the amount of time students spend in the classroom. But such discussions help us to understand the process of language learning in children.)

An effective way to plan programs for children is to look closely at what they are able to do at various stages. The five- to seven-year-olds can talk about activities; they can relay details of past activities, and they can discuss what they are going to do or would like to do. They have a degree of reasoning ability and they can take clear directions. Their greatest asset is imagination. They also need to feel safe and they need to change activities as their concentration wanes. They learn by listening, looking, and touching. They can associate ideas, though they do not always understand the associations. They respond well when there is clear logic involved in an activity.

Most often, as children move beyond seven, they are becoming much clearer about what they think; they can make more clear-cut decisions, and their opinions are more firm. They ask endless questions and are now able to question the intentions of those around them, including their teachers. They want things to be fair and they can focus on goals for success. Children of seven to eleven or twelve have extended attention spans, but they still need variety. They are becoming better at working together on projects with other children, and they are becoming more sensitive to possible failure.

With these characteristics in mind, we can plan lessons that are most effective. Draw from the energy and enthusiasm of the young students, and provide them opportunity to use their imaginations and their desire to succeed. Do everything possible to eliminate the fear of failure issues, and allow them to have fun.

One basic technique for the very young learners is "teach, play, teach, play." Plan activities that have a component of demonstrating new material, then quickly bring in a game that reinforces the material. As you teach, you will learn to keep children active and involved so that they can learn and so that they can be managed. As they get older, they can work alone in longer blocks of time. You will learn to alternate "alone study time" with group interactivity. Children and adults have many characteristics in common: They need intrinsic motivation and they usually learn well in interactive situations. However, there are some important differences. Adult have life experience on which they can build. Children are getting their foundation in education as they are learning the language. English must be an integral part of their total learning experience. Adults generally know what is best for them, but children do not. They cannot decide for themselves what they need to learn.

Visuals are helpful on any level, and with children they are essential. If you have experience working with children, you already know what attracts children. If you do not, then it will serve you well to get some experience by volunteering or, at the very least, through observing classrooms. Remember that your goal is to facilitate their learning of English, and your daily objective is to keep children involved and happy. For that reason, structure, variety, and fun are crucial elements on your lesson planning. Plan each lesson with those things in mind, and set up a safe learning atmosphere for your students. And have fun!

A Multifaceted Approach

You may find yourself planning your lessons rather instinctively as you focus on your students' needs and interests. You may try various approaches without consciously considering what they are based on, and for the most part, that is fine. At some point, you may need to justify your approach to the organization with which you are associated, or you may simply want to satisfy your own curiosity about how different approaches work. Let's take a close look at three general categories of teaching approaches: conversational, problem-solving, and grammar-based.

A conversation approach lends itself well to an interactive style of teaching. An instructor can rather easily plan lessons on conversation models that will work the student through the life topics. The primary challenge is to get the best angle on each topic so that you are tapping the learners' intrinsic motivation. A problem-solving approach has an inherent technique of provoking, and provocation is a great motivation. Interactivity is natural when people are working to find a solution to a problem, even when it is a hypothetical one. A grammar-based approach can assure the instructor that a firm foundation is being put in place for the students' grasp of how the elements of the language work within language structure. Each approach has strengths, and as each stands alone, it has its own sets of weaknesses. Conversation alone doesn't ensure that building blocks are being put in place; problem-solving can be highly motivating, and yet it does not promise to cover the essential topics. (Some topics aren't easily handled as problems.) A purely grammar-based approach always runs the risk of becoming downright boring. A skillful balance of various approaches, however, is ideal.

The following models are offered to illustrate how you might begin with a conversation approach then incorporate a grammar-based approach: If you were teaching the words *decide* and *decided*, you could begin your presentation by establishing some things that we might decide to do. You will notice that we've quickly moved into the use of *to* with an infinitive: *to do: decided to do.* As you build up a conversation model, add in the grammar pattern: *My sister decided to stop smoking.* Now we've also moved into gerund usage: *smoking.* It is likely that you will have touched on such usage before you get to this particular lesson and that's fine, because now you can build on the students' familiarity with the elements of grammar.

Starter model:

A. Guess what my sister decided to do?
B. I can't imagine. Tell me!
A. She decided to quit smoking.
B. That's interesting. Is she going to quit immediately?

Continue working with the model by changing out key words and phrases: *Guess* *what / sister / I can't imagine /quit / smoking, That's interesting / immediately.*

A. You won't believe what my <u>father</u> <u>decided to do</u>.
B. I have no idea. Please tell me.
A. He <u>decided to start playing</u> golf.
B. You're kidding. <u>Is</u> he <u>going to start</u> this spring?

After the model with its change-outs becomes comfortable, you can substitute the primary grammar pattern: *decided to do* and *use plans to do,* or *wants to do*

A. Let me tell you what my wife <u>plans to do</u> this year.
B. Oh, please do. I'll bet it's something interesting.
A. She<u>'s planning to go</u> on a cruise to South America.
B. Wow! I wish I could afford to do that.

Consider all the change-outs that you can now work with.

A. Bet you can't guess what my friend and <u>I are thinking of doing</u>.
B. I haven't a clue.
A. We<u>'re thinking about going</u> to New York.
B. That's great. Will your friends mind if <u>I decide to go</u> too?

As you can see, these little models can take you and your students through a lot of material and variations of grammar elements and patterns, all with a conversational approach. Once you have established a basic understanding of those elements involved in your lesson, write them on the board or on a handout.

After you have worked your way through a series of sessions, you will have a feeling for how the elements work and how quickly or how slowly they need to be worked in order to meet certain objectives. Once you become comfortable with conversation models, you will find it easy to set goals for building language structure and for covering life topics and to build lesson plans from one session to another.

A problem-solving approach to lesson can be quite a motivating way to present material and to work in important issues of language structure. The primary format is one of problem/solution. The lesson begins with someone mentioning a problem. Students are then compelled to help him or her find a solution, and that will mean struggling to master new words, sentence structure, and language strategies to do so.

Conversation model:

A. A tree fell on my house and I don't know what to do about it.
B. Tell me when it happened and how.
A. That storm last night and the terrible wind.
B. Did it cause a lot of damage?
A. Sure did.
B. You need to call your insurance company right away.

This model is perfect for moving intermediate or advanced students quickly into free conversation. It is also a great way to build a repertoire of expressions.

Take a close look at the sentence structures first, then at the expressions:

Compound sentence: *A tree fell on my house* and *I don't know what to do about it.*
A sentence pattern within a sentence: *Tell me when it happened and how.*
Sentence fragments: *That storm last night and that terrible wind.*
Expressions: *It sure did. Right away.*

Add more problem-solving topics to the following list:

occupational hazards
management and supervisors concerns
paycheck errors
Misunderstandings between co-workers

strategies for job searches
family conflicts

Add some starters for problem presentation:

What should I do if . . . ?
Have you ever had a problem with . . . ?
How should I handle . . . ?

A grammar approach is greatly enhanced by adding techniques of conversation and problem-solving. Create model conversations as springboards for strong lessons. Add in some problem-solving strategies. Keep conversations going by allowing students to participate fully, yet be sure to hold enough control so that the class can cover the necessities and not go too far off the subject. Remember always to plan interactive lessons with your students' needs and interests in mind. Use a protocol to create a bit of formality, and always remain flexible. As you gain experience in teaching, you become comfortable planning lessons with a variety of techniques and approaches, and your students will benefit from your skills.

Building Courses of Study

In this unit:

- A Plan to Keep You in Line
- Structure and Flexibility
- Specialty and Specialization Courses
- Model Courses of Study
- Put It in Writing and Word It Well

A Plan to Keep You in Line

*C*urriculum—the very word can be scary to those who have public or private school teaching experience, especially if you've had to "make up" course outlines to appease some "higher-ups," knowing all the while that you would have to depart from the arbitrary constraints of the written plan as soon as you got into the real teaching situation. While you know that a "course of action"—let's call it that—can be a great aid as you are wading through elements of topics day by day, it helps to think it all out beforehand, and then set it forth on paper and say: *There, I now know what I'm planning to do . . . sort of.*

Curriculum has that Latin sound to it that smacks of academia, and to those of you who've never been introduced to issues of education in an academic setting, that very word, along with other Greek-based words such as *pedagogy* can make you feel as though you are out of your element. But that needn't be so. Just think of it as a plan, a course of study, a written guide to aid you and to sort of keep you in line. You will reap the benefits of having that guide nearby as you do daily lesson plans. Your curriculum will help you to stay on track so that you are confident you are incorporating all the elements needed to move your students on to the next level.

Structure and Flexibility

Just as in your daily lessons, the structure in your curriculum planning comes easily from goals and objectives -- those that you have decided your students need in order to move to the next level, whatever that might be. For example: if you are in a program with several levels and your class is going on to level three after your course, you can determine what material should be sandwiched between levels one and three, then divvy it up by the number of session in your course. That sounds easy enough. But, of course, we all know of the "plans of mice and men" (Nothing ever seems to work as we suppose it might, at least not until you have some experience behind you so that you can gauge how things might go.) Your course of study will have structure, yet give allowance for flexibility for whatever might come. It would work the same way even

---

if you were planning a course for tutoring one or two people, or for a small group of employees. In those situations you probably wouldn't be sandwiched between other levels, and you would have to draw from common sense and logic as to what topics you could cover.

Here is an interesting paradox: You are often expected to create the course of study before the course begins, yet you cannot have a full picture of who your students will be and what their needs and interests are before they are in front of you. (Remember that this all becomes easier with experience.) But you can be certain of a few things: All students tap into issues of the life topics. The only question now is which issues and with what angle, and how much time will they need to exhaust the issues to their satisfaction?

You can always turn to a good set of textbooks for a look at what is often being taught on a particular level. Just take care that if the texts were designed for a certain group of students -- such as a large multicultural classroom -- and you've found yourself teaching a group of six Chinese teens, you'll surely need to hone the issues to the teens' interests and needs. The basic topic and, to some degree, the angle on the issues will be the same.

In a multicultural class of adults, I would want to use material relating to rental property or buying homes under the general topic of housing. However, for six Chinese teens, I would shift to issues that relate to the younger single culture. A Chinese teenager is most likely living at home with parents. He or she may be interested in whether or not the other students have their own bedrooms, or share with siblings. Room arrangements might be of interest. Perhaps a computer is in one young person's room and a TV in another. With teens, you can always work from their motivation to aspire to young adulthood. Questions: *Do you plan to have your own apartment when you begin to earn an income, or if you go away to college? Would you rather live in an apartment in a large city or a subdivision in a suburb? Why? Are houses different in this state than houses in, say New York, Hong Kong, Singapore, or Taiwan?* Of course, you will not know their responses until you are in the classroom; but, as you are creating your plan of study, you could schedule in a session on "Housing" with several focal points, and then allow the session to take its natural course. That is the sort of flexibility you need.

Specialty and Specialization Courses

Teaching English for specific reasons is coming into vogue, creating specialization courses, and they can focus on a particular field or subject such as business English, landscaping, restaurants, medical, computers and internet technology, or perhaps travel and tourism. Or, they can be designed as a specialty course to meets the needs of a particular group of people. Sometimes a group of people of the same culture and language desire a course that is focused on their needs, which might be a particular age group, religion, neighborhood, or hobby. The possibilities for specialization are endless. It is simply a matter of finding a group of people who are interested in the same area of study. Or, perhaps, it is easier to let them find one another. For example, you might run an inexpensive ad in your local newspaper -- assuming you live in an area that has a sizable international community -- to see if there is an interest in a particular specialty. The ad could be rather generic, something such as: *Will teach advanced English to small group in your home or mine.* Or, an ad might read, *Refine your English! Interactive classes in the home.*

It is not unusual that someone of a particular language -- let's say Japanese, just for an example -- sees the ad and talks it over with a few friends. You might get a phone call from that woman, telling you that she and her friends are wondering how much you would charge. That's certainly a good question. If you have already gained a bit of experience and you feel confident about jumping head-on into the situation, then you could charge whatever is the going rate in your area. As you get more acquainted with others teachers, you will get a feel for rates. They go up with the rest of the economy.

What exactly would be the "specialty" around which you would build the course for the Japanese women? This is something you can establish with your new students. Find out as much as possible as you talk with the woman who contacted you. What sorts of topics are she and her friends interested in? What levels are they? How long did they study English in Japan? In the US? Ask plenty of questions. You will learn precisely what the women are interested in as you go into the course; but the basics will be pronunciation, conversation, idioms, and polite protocol of daily activities.

Japanese speakers have a particular set of pronunciation difficulties, which you will discover rather quickly. You might find that they are well-educated in English but haven't had much experience in speaking. Conversation must then be at the forefront of each lesson. Such students often need only the opportunity of a safe environment in which to practice their conversation. Also, they will be happy to have the mysteries solved of those crazy-sounding idioms that pepper American English. They particularly enjoy learning how to handle daily situations: how to talk with their children's teachers, what questions to ask, how to negotiate with service people, and how to say no politely. People will join such a group and continue on for as long as it is feasible. Often they will refer friends to their teacher, and new groups will form. Before you know it, your little part-time job can turn into serious business. Specialty courses can be centered on any topic. Some groups of people are interested in learning about a religion or about a certain set of doctrine within a religion. The instructor would, of course, need to know that field of religion fairly well in order to conduct such classes.

Many entry-level jobs are open to limited-English speakers who then find themselves struggling to communicate, for example: the assistants in a nursing home or hospital. They are stuck in the lowest of jobs until they can communicate well enough to work more effectively with patients and staff. They need the jargon of the business. Some facilities are happy to contract with a teacher who can help. This specialty course would be centered on the terminology conversation needed for basic communication.

Specialization courses arise wherever there is a need. Just a few examples would be: English for Restaurant Employees, English for Retail Sales (department store employees), English for Preschoolers, Accent Reduction for Asians (or anyone else), Tourism English (travel), and TOFEL Prep Specialist (preparing people to take the exam needed for entrance into college). You name it and there's probably a need somewhere. Many people simply do not have the time to spend on building a proper foundation for their English, yet they desperately need quick English for a specific need. Build courses that work, and then expand your clientele and become a specialist in the areas that appeal to you most.

If your class is interested in business English, it might be assumed that they have already mastered the rudiments of the language enough to attempt to communicate in the business world. What they want and need is specific terminology, and refinement of language strategies and of pronunciation. Your lesson plans must reflect those areas. Be sure to divvy up your sessions to address all three. A daily segment for terminology might be a good starting place; it will get the students mentally involved quickly. Be sure to bring yourself up to speed on business English, and incorporate as many modern issues and terms and phrases as possible.

A discussion of how people in business do and say things might be in second order. That can be an endless subject with segments on idioms, trendy words and phrases, and on business protocol. Then, thirdly, focus on specific pronunciation problems. At this level of pronunciation refinement, you will want to educate yourself well on the reasons that certain people have certain problems. Sometimes simply talking about those reasons can be helpful to the participants. Those coming from extremely tonal languages, such as Chinese and Vietnamese, have difficulty relaxing their control of intonation. That's what tends to make them sound mechanical or choppy. Spend a lot of time with intonation as you might if you were teaching musical scales. Talk about the ways that we use intonation to change meaning. *(That's my book you have there.* The implication is that it's *that* item rather than another. *That's my book you have there.* The emphasis on *my* can sound accusatory.)

Spend ample time discussing the ways in which we communicate through our choices of expression and of intonation. *(Yes, I would like to go with you. Sure, I'll go with you. Yes, I'd like to go with you. I'd like very much to join you. Yeah, I'll go.)* How many different ways can we express a desire to go with someone, or how many ways can we say something to imply that we are going only out of duty? It is interesting how much business English has to do with language strategy. That fact can give your lessons a focal point.

Many specialty courses can be taught in community centers, churches, businesses, and schools. However, if you find yourself running a teaching business out of your home, take all necessary steps to handle it as a business. That would include getting proper insurance so that you are covered in the event that someone is injured on your property. If a business license is required, then get one. Remember that business expenses can be tax deductions. Oh, and don't forget to pay taxes on your earnings!

Model Courses of Study

The following are some examples of course outlines, overviews, and summaries, which you might find helpful when planning curriculum for survival, beginning, intermediate, advanced, enrichment levels, and tutoring, as well as a course of study for teaching specialty and specialization courses. I have mixed them up so to offer you samples of two, four, and five days per week sessions, but any of the courses can fall into any of the schedules. It is just a matter of your adjusting the materials to fit the schedules.

Survival Level	
This 12-week, 48-session course is designed to establish a foundation of vocabulary, pronunciation, and recognition of words and sounds of English so speakers are able to move onto Level One ESL.	
The focus is on:	
✓ identification of basic vocabulary relating to the life topics	
✓ with exercises in simple sentence patterns using affirmative, negative, and interrogative forms.	
✓ practice drills in simple conversation and pronunciation will be a strong component of the course.	
Schedule: Mondays, Tuesdays, Wednesdays, Thursdays 6 p.m. to 9 p.m.	
Week One (Survival level)	
Monday	greetings, personal information (name, address, phone numbers)
Tuesday	identification of items in the classroom
Wednesday	colors and numbers
Thursday	people (man, woman, child) in singular and plural

Week Two (Survival level)	
Monday	telling time
Tuesday	identifying foods and categories of foods
Wednesday	buying foods
Thursday	identifying money
Friday	review

Week Three (Survival level)	
Monday	now, every day, and yesterday with basic verbs (eat, study, etc.)
Tuesday	days and telling time
Wednesday	identifying foods
Thursday	identifying occupations (work titles)

Week Four (Survival level)	
Monday	identifying body parts
Tuesday	expressing emotions (happy, sad, and so forth)
Wednesday	expressing pain or sickness
Thursday	answering the question: What's the matter?

Week Five (Survival level)	
Monday	review of *now*, *every day* and *yesterday* with basic verbs (eat, drink, study, talk, work), days and telling time, identifying foods, identifying occupations (work titles)
Tuesday	review of family relationships (mother, father, brother, sister, grandparents), recognizing written and spoken numbers, identifying numbers on a clock, identifying denominations of money
Wednesday	review of daily activities, days and telling time, identifying and buying foods, counting money and making change
Thursday	review of body parts, expressing emotions (happy, sad, and so forth), expressing pain or sickness, answering the question: What's the matter?

Week Six (Survival level)	
Monday	buses, planes, trains, and cars
Tuesday	traffic signals
Wednesday	Maps
Thursday	giving directions, action words -- now, yesterday, every day, tomorrow.
Week Seven (Survival level)	
Monday	calling 911
Tuesday	Identifying household objects
Wednesday	Identifying household furnishings
Thursday	Identifying food in the refrigerator and cabinets
Week Eight (Survival level)	
Monday	names of jobs
Tuesday	work actions
Wednesday	tools and equipment
Thursday	jobs ads
Week Nine (Survival level)	
Monday	Introducing others
Tuesday	preparing food
Wednesday	going to the market_
Thursday	finding what you need
Week Ten (Survival level)	
Monday	review of buses, planes, trains, and cars, traffic signals, maps, giving directions, action words -- now, yesterday, every day, tomorrow
Tuesday	review calling 911, identifying household objects, identifying household furnishings, identifying food in the refrigerator and cabinets
Wednesday	review names of jobs, work actions, tools and equipment, jobs ads
Thursday	review of all of Week Ten topics
Week Eleven (Survival level)	
Monday	identify clothing
Tuesday	clothing sizes

Wednesday	practice too big, too small, and fits
Thursday	asking the question: How much does it cost?

Week Twelve (Survival level)	
Monday	helping people
Tuesday	eating in a restaurant
Wednesday	reading menus
Thursday	action words (*now, yesterday, every day, and tomorrow*)

Week Thirteen (Survival level)	
Monday	having fun
Tuesday	leisure activities
Wednesday	answering the question: What do you want?
Thursday	action words (*now, yesterday, every day, and tomorrow*)

Week Fourteen (Survival level)	
Monday	talking about your family
Tuesday	family activities
Wednesday	answering the question: What do you like?
Thursday	action words (*now, yesterday, every day, and tomorrow*)

Week Fifteen (Survival level)	
Monday	review of clothing, clothing sizes, and *too big, too small*, and *fits*; asking the question: *How much does it cost?*
Tuesday	helping people; eating in a restaurant; reading menus; action words (*now, yesterday, every day, and tomorrow*)
Wednesday	continued review and assessment
Thursday	continued review and assessment

Beginning Level

This four-month 60-session course is offered Monday through Thursday evening from 6 to 9 p.m., beginning January 12 and ending May 11.

The course is designed for students who have basic survival skills, which include the ability to write the alphabet and sound out the letters; familiarity with numbers, dates, months, and basic vocabulary relating to life topics; and the ability to recognize simple sentence structures in affirmative, negative, and interrogative. The goal of the course is to build on those survival skills so that the student will increase his or her command of vocabulary, pronunciation, sentence structure, and conversation in order to move on to the intermediate level.

Topics include:

- ✓ interacting with people
- ✓ working
- ✓ shopping
- ✓ foods
- ✓ housing
- ✓ recreation
- ✓ health and emergencies

Week One (Beginning level)

Monday	greetings, personal information (name, address, phone number)
Tuesday	classroom, home, and family (names and items)
Wednesday	numbers and days of the week
Thursday	months and seasons
Friday	review

Week Two (Beginning level)

Monday	telling time
Tuesday	identifying foods and categories of foods
Wednesday	buying foods

Thursday	identifying money
Friday	review

Week Three (Beginning level)	
Monday	daily activities
Tuesday	days and telling time
Wednesday	identifying and buying foods
Thursday	counting money and making change
Friday	review

Week Four (Beginning level)	
Monday	identifying aches, pains, symptoms, and body parts
Tuesday	making medical appointments
Wednesday	talking to the doctor
Thursday	calling in to work sick
Friday	review

Week Five (Beginning level)	
Monday	identifying means of transportation
Tuesday	going places near home
Wednesday	getting and giving directions
Thursday	getting and giving directions
Friday	review

Week Six (Beginning level)	
Monday	review of greetings, personal information (name, address, phone number); classroom, home, and family (names and items); numbers and days of the week; months and seasons
Tuesday	telling time, foods and categories of foods, buying foods, money
Wednesday	daily activities, days and telling time, identifying and buying foods, counting money, and making change
Thursday	aches, pains, symptoms, and body parts, making medical appointments, talking to the doctor, calling in to work sick
Friday	means of transportation, going place near home, going far from home, giving directions
Week Seven (Beginning level)	
Monday	emergency information, identifying yourself and others
Tuesday	reading classified ads for rentals
Wednesday	identifying rooms in houses and apartments
Thursday	calling on the phone to ask a question
Friday	review
Week Eight (Beginning level)	
Monday	occupations
Tuesday	workplaces
Wednesday	Tools and equipment
Thursday	Work procedures
Friday	review
Week Nine (Beginning level)	
Monday	social activities and recreation
Tuesday	holidays and celebrations

Wednesday	food preparation
Thursday	favorite pastimes and hobbies
Friday	review

Week Ten (Beginning level)

Monday	reporting problems on the job
Tuesday	reporting problems to a landlord
Wednesday	opening a bank account and depositing money
Thursday	writing checks
Friday	review

Week Eleven (Beginning level)

Monday	clothing
Tuesday	selecting sizes and trying on clothes
Wednesday	making purchases
Thursday	likes and dislikes in food, clothing, recreation, sports
Friday	review

Week Twelve (Beginning level)

Monday	review of emergency information, identifying yourself and others; identifying rooms in houses and apartments; reading classified ads for rentals; calling on the phone to ask a question
Tuesday	review of occupations, work places, tools and equipment, work procedures
Wednesday	social activities and recreation, holidays and celebrations, food preparations, favorite pastimes and hobbies
Thursday	reporting problems on the job, reporting problems to a landlord, opening a bank account and depositing money, writing checks

Friday	Clothing; selecting sizes and trying on clothes; purchasing with checks, cash, and credit; likes and dislikes in food, clothing, recreation, sports

Intermediate Level

This is a 12-week grammar-based conversation course designed for the student who has:

- ✓ satisfactorily completed a beginning level or who has pasted a placement test for intermediate level

- ✓ a strong base of vocabulary, an beginning mastery of the sound system of English and of simple and compound sentence structures

- ✓ the ability to work with model conversations.

Week One	<ul><li>A review of all beginning elements, including simple and continuous tenses, subject and object pronouns, and possessive adjectives.</li><li>An introduction to perfect tenses.</li></ul>
Week Two	<ul><li>Lessons that integrate simple, continuous, and perfect tenses.</li><li>An introduction to continuous perfect tenses.</li></ul>
Week Three	<ul><li>Introduction of gerunds and infinitives.</li><li>Review of present perfect and present perfect continuous tenses.</li></ul>
Week Four	<ul><li>Introduction to past perfect and past perfect continuous tenses.</li><li>Review of all previously learned tenses.</li></ul>
Week Five	<ul><li>Introduction to gerunds and infinitives.</li><li>Review of past perfect and past perfect continuous tenses.</li></ul>

Week Six	• Review of gerunds and infinitives. • Introduction of passive voice.
Week Seven	• Introduction of modals (should, must, might, may, could). • Review of passive voice.
Week Eight	• Review of modals. • Introduction of conditional sentence structures with clauses, real and unreal.
Week Nine	• Review of real versus unreal (hypothetical) clauses. • Continued introduction to conditional unreal present tense.
Week Ten	• Review of conditional unreal present tense. • Continued introduction of conditional, with past tense.
Week Eleven	• Review of present and past tense conditional • Begin review of all intermediate grammar from previous lessons.
Week Twelve	• Continued review of all intermediate grammar from previous lessons.

Advanced Level

This course is designed for the student who has at least mastered intermediate skills in pronunciation, sentence structure, and vocabulary. The course contains 24 sessions, and meets twice a week for four hours for 12 weeks. The goal is to guide the student to obtain approximately 70% of the language (for successful communication in the community and on most jobs).

Each session focuses on:

- ✓ language strategies (the various ways of expressing oneself for effective communication and for free conversation)

- ✓ pronunciation

- ✓ correct grammar

Topics are those of the interest to the participants, including:

- ✓ issues of the community

- ✓ the workplace

- ✓ consumerism and finance

- ✓ friends and family

- ✓ schools

This level provides:

- ✓ pre-assessment and post-assessment

- ✓ homework assignments

- ✓ after-class assistance

- ✓ individual tutoring arranged for an additional fee

A sample daily agenda is as follows:

1. pronunciation drills (15 minutes)

2. modeled and free conversation for language strategies on selected topics (2 hours)

3. break (15 minutes)

4. pronunciation and sentence structure drills (15 minutes)

5. grammar review (45 minutes)

6. free conversation (one hour)

Enrichment Level

An Overview:

A course for those who function well in the English language but feel they need refinement in the areas of language strategies and pronunciation. Each session is total teacher and student interactivity and includes practice with idioms and expressions unique to American English, a strong focus on refinement of pronunciation, and conversation related to topics of interest to the participants. Class meets for two and a half hours, two afternoons per week during each school semester. Though the class meets in the school, anyone -- in addition to parents -- is invited.

Business English

This course is for professionals who need to improve English skills for success in the business world. Each session will focus on language strategies, expressions, and terminology for business, with a question-and-answer period to discuss participant interests and concerns. Classes will meet twice a week for two hours for five weeks. The following topics are included: business letters, reports, memorandums, e-mail correspondence, legal documentation, proper resource citations, meetings, agendas, business/social protocol, presentations, business travel, general business terminology and profession-specific jargon, taboos, necessities, ethics, and regulatory issues.

Tutoring

Is in nearly impossible to map out a detailed curriculum for tutoring a single student, but surely an outline of topics and a summary of approach will make both the student and the tutor feel more confident. The great things about tutoring are that you must work at the pace of the individual, and you don't have other students pulling forward or holding back. It is still important that you determine the student's foundation, and then that you cover the essentials to move him or her forward a higher level, whatever that might be. Work from the life topics to create angles that will have an appeal the student. If the student is in high school and new to the US, you might do a unit entitled, *How fast is fast food?* rather than one on shopping at the market. You can easily make up arbitrary names for each lesson, then work from questions such as *Where do the kids in your class eat when they go out together?* From that discussion of food, you can move easily into social conversation, which you might entitle *Fast Talk*.

If you are tutoring someone in their home, you might make a visit first to note the manner in which the student lives so that you can come up with topics that directly relate the his or her lifestyle. The tutoring curriculum will seem much more flexible than one designed for a formal classroom; therefore, it will be wise to follow some sort of structure from a text so that you don't skip over important language structure elements. Hand out the course outline to the student, just as you would to a class of students. He or she can look ahead and anticipate the upcoming lessons.

Industrial Contract Training
English in the Workplace: A Course for XYZ Employees
Summer Course, 12 weeks, 2 sessions per week, 2 hours per session
JUNE
Session 1 (Introductions of participants, instructor, and material to be covered, and pre-assessment) Lesson: Identification of tools and equipment (visuals or actual items)
Session 2 Lesson: Purpose of tools and equipment (a forklift is for moving large items)
Session 3 Lesson: Locating tools and equipment (Where is the drill?)
Session 4 Lesson: Review identification of tools and equipment and sentence structures for purpose and location of item
Session 5 Lesson: Locations within the plant, warehouse, or store (Where's a water fountain?)
Session 6 Lesson: Identification of job titles (John is our foreman.)
Session 7 Lesson: Locations of jobs within the company (Check out your tools in the Equipment Department)
Session 8 Lesson: Review of identification and locations
JULY
Session 9 Lesson: *When* questions (When can I pick up my check?)
Session 10 Lesson: Using tools and equipment (Please show me how to operate the _____.)
Session 11 Lesson: Communicating with fellow employees (What department are you in?)

Session 12 Lesson: Review of "when" questions, using tools and equipment, and communicating with fellow employees
Session 13 Lesson: Working together (Please hand me the drill!)
Session 14 Lesson: Asking for help (Could you give me a hand here?)
Session 15 Lesson: Understanding rules and regulations
Session 16 Lesson: Review all topics
AUGUST
Session 17 Lesson: Working efficiently (Is there an easier way to do this?)
Session 18 Lesson: Moving up in your job (How do I get a promotion?)
Session 19 Lesson: Qualifications
Session 20 Lesson: Review of working efficiently, moving up in your job, and qualifications
Session 21 Lessons: Explaining procedures, and communicating well
Session 22 Lesson: Complete sentences and fragments, American slang and contractions
Session 23 Lesson: Review of all lessons (How can I learn more English?)
Session: 24 Lesson: Post assessment

Put It in Writing, and Word It Well!

As you are finalizing your written course of study, work in a revision draft that will permit you to bring it to its optimum potential, if you need to share with anyone and especially if it will be a source for evaluation later. I suggest that you go through a check list to see that the curriculum is worded so that it will not lock you into something impossible, and so that it is attractive and appealing to those who view it. All of your written plans are part of your professional image. Remember that the curriculum is generally composed for three reasons: to demonstrate to the organization for which you are teaching that you do have a plan to perform; to give the student an idea of where they will be going; and last but not at all the least, to keep you in line and on target. Having the written course of study as a guide will take a lot of pressure off you so that you can concentrate your energies into the day- by-day instruction.

The check list is as follows:
✓ Does the written curriculum identify and describe the course (course title schedule and overview)?
✓ Have you included the necessary topics?
✓ Does the outline make your approach clear (conversational, grammar-based, competency, or multifaceted, and so forth)?
✓ Does the outline reveal that you are working from intrinsic motivation and that the sessions will be interactive?
✓ Is the terminology enticing, yet general enough that you will not later find yourself defending it?
✓ Does it, in one glance, look like a comprehensive course of study for the purpose?

Establishing Yourself as an Instructor of English to Speakers of Other Languages

In this unit:

- Steps to Professionalism
- Your Resumes
- Contracts
- Growing Programs Naturally
- Teaching in Other Countries
- Protecting Your Materials

Steps to Professionalism

Confidence, know-how, and experience are three components that will move you forward in any venture. As you are acquiring and refining those qualifications, it is important that you also learn how to promote them by allowing your confidence to come through in all of your contacts, by articulating your know-how, and by exhibiting your experience. Once you have decided that you want to teach English to speakers of other languages, it is time to start working on those three components. Begin by understanding that teaching language is a natural act. Your confidence will build as you dispel all the myths about how people learn, and as you minimize the academic jargon and think in terms of what is truly effective. Common sense and a desire to work with people are the necessary ingredients for developing skills. If you have both qualities, nothing should be allowed to stand in your way. Thus, your confidence will grow.

Know-how comes, in part, through study, and you will want to learn much more as you go along. Continue to pry into and question each of the areas that were presented in the book:
✓ Who and where are students and teachers of ESL?
✓ How is language acquired?
✓ How do intrinsic motivation and interactivity work?
✓ How are TPR, PPP, and other techniques best implemented?
✓ Where can texts and materials be found?
✓ How are interactive lessons built?
✓ What are the barriers to learning in culturally diverse situations, and how can they be broken down?
✓ How are student and teacher goals set and met?
✓ How are curricula and programs developed?

The components of *know-how*, of course, come through experience. Gain experience however and wherever possible! Be careful not to take on too much. Teaching English to speakers of other languages can be great fun, but it is also an emotionally and physically demanding activity. Try all sorts of things at first to see what you enjoy the most, including: volunteer tutoring, assisting in established programs even when the salary is lower, or creating a class within your current position by designing a course based on needs and interests. The rest is simply a matter of learning how to develop rapport with people as they move into the role of students. Once you have some experience and your confidence has grown a bit, try designing a course for a local business, church, or community center (the needs are everywhere). Allow the program to grow naturally, and then expand into other areas. You will soon realize you have discovered a lot about how people learn, what motivates them to continue, and how programs grow.

Self-Promotion

Now you will be ready to create business cards and a strong resume and learn how to put together an effective course proposal. Of course, you may have already gotten business cards, and then after a bit of experience realized the information needs to be more specific to the areas to which you are drawn (English for Internationals, American English for Japanese, English for Better Business, English Activities for Preschoolers, English for Parents of American Schoolchildren, and so forth). Put a title after your name: "Instructor of English to Speakers of Other Languages" or "Instructor of English for Internationals." Be sure you add your e-mail address. Try to come up with a slogan that will make the business card appear active ("Interactive Learning," "English at your own pace!" or whatever.) It is good to invest a little money for sharper-looking cards. It does make a difference. Study the quality carefully before choosing paper, print, and style.

Your Resume

Your resume is important. Keep in mind that people do not always read such documents thoroughly; however, they do get impressions from them. Your resume should be professional, but not dull. It should be interesting and eye-catching, yet not flashy. Make it concise and clear so that a person can glance at it and see that you are a forthright person who wants and intends to do a good job. Every time you approach an organization about designing a course, be prepared to present your business card, resume, and eventually a course proposal.

Proposals

A course proposal may seem complex, but it is simply a written extension of your initial conversation with the representative of the organization. In your approach, you will state verbally that you see a need for English courses and that you can meet that need. A proposal is simply the written continuation of that discussion, a conversation that would go something like this: "I realize that your company (or community, church, etc.) has some language needs. I know this because I specialize in the area of English for speakers of other languages. I have know-how and experience in the field, and I can help you." The steps to creating a great proposal are built on those statements (know-how and willingness to meet the need), by elaborating each issue in a way that gives the person a wake-up call that there is a concern for communication within his or her business, church, or community.

You probably can find a proposal model somewhere on your computer software. If not, simply begin by writing a brief *overview* of what you intend to do—something along these lines: "The following is a proposal and plan for establishing a course of English for speakers of other languages for XYZ employees. The goal is to design the course specifically for the company's needs and interests so that the participants will improve their level of effective communication." Of course you can expand upon those ideas, but keep the overview brief.

Following the overview, you will need to explain to the company or organization exactly why such a course is important. This is the *rationale*, and its goal is to help management realize that there is a need, and that the company will benefit from your services. A good strong paragraph will do, unless more is needed to get the point across.

Just after the rationale, talk about yourself and your qualifications in a written conversational way. Your resume should be attached, but remember that people do not read resumes thoroughly. Take the opportunity in the proposal to tell the reader who you are and why you can do the job. Perhaps one paragraph will be enough. If you want to title it, you might call it *Instructor's Background*. You needn't list specific items the way you would on the resume; rather, summarize your experience, your interest, and your ambition to do a good job and to help people with communication.

Finally, the proposal should have a *plan of action*: a fairly detailed explanation of how many sessions there will be, the length of each session, when you prefer to run the course (months, days, and time). Give a list of the topics you plan to cover, keeping it general so that you can make changes according to the way things go. Explain, in general terms, what materials and techniques you will use. Though these elements might not mean much to management, they show that you are serious and that you have thought the course out as much as possible (before doing a pre-assessment). Add a final sentence that allows you some flexibility: something like "All materials and techniques will be used with the approval of the company and according to their effectiveness in each given situation."

Review and revise the proposal until it reads smoothly and clearly. Try to read it objectively, as though you are the person who will make the final decision about whether or not to accept it. Revise it to make it interesting and vital. Make sure the sentences flow nicely and the words and style are accessible to the average reader.

Contracts

When you have gotten a proposal accepted, draw up a simple contract that will be attached to the proposal. Make a statement in the contract that the proposal is an addendum and that the contract is based on that proposal. Usually you can assume that you will be paid for your teaching once the course is complete, though there is never a guarantee that any contract will hold up in court if there is a misinterpretation about the proposed or executed job. Write the contract carefully and clearly so that there is not a likelihood of a problem. Be careful not to make statements such as: "Every person will know all of the material." *You can never keep a promise like that.* If the written word backs up all that you and the manager have said, there should not be a problem. Be sure your fee and the costs of materials are itemized and that the terms of payment are made clear. Often the intentions of managers are good, but there needs to be follow-through by the payroll department. Make certain everything is in writing and that details, including the time of payment, have been thoroughly discussed.

Growing Programs Naturally

Once you have become involved in contract work through any organization, you will find that interest and courses grow naturally. Think in terms of building a foundation of knowledge in each situation. Doing so will help you create levels. For example: You might teach a 10- or 12-week course that meets twice a week. As you near the end of the course, find out if participants are interested in learning more. (Usually they will tell you before you have a chance to ask.) As you offer more first-level courses, the number of interested persons will grow. Of course, some will feel they cannot keep up with classes, but do not feel bad about that. Encourage them to continue at a later date or to repeat a course; then concentrate on the needs of the people who are anxious to move forward. Don't be disappointed if this growth doesn't take place the first few times you run a course.

**It may take a while to build momentum,
to gain and to exhibit your confidence and expertise.**

When a program grows naturally, it tends to be a much stronger than when people try to push up the numbers of participants. Word-of-mouth spreads quickly. Before long the classes will become larger, and that will allow you more possibilities for splitting groups into levels, thus growing a program. You will need to continuously re-evaluate your pre- and post-assessments, your plans of study and lesson plans, as well as your knowledge. Also, you should expect to raise your fee as numbers of students increase and as you gain more experience and credibility.

**There is no limit to what you can do once things get rolling—
if you truly enjoy teaching.**

Business opportunities exist in abundance to anyone with an adventurous spirit, and teaching English to speakers of other languages can be quite an entrepreneurial venture. However, it is important for you to look at the instruction from both sides: that of the instructor and of the person or organization paying the bills, providing the location, buying the textbooks, and paying your salary. A wise businessperson learns to think like the contractors as well as the people with whom that contract is being made. When a company, church, or any sort of benefactor puts up money to get a program started and/or to keep it going, the people behind the money have definite reasons and goals. It is crucial that we try our best to understand just what those reasons and goals are, even when they do not seem to be totally in line with our own.

A large discount store begins to hire limited-English speakers and the personnel department soon finds that there is a concern for communication and a strong possibility of losing business because of the problem. The decision-makers within that company know it is important that the store show interest in the limited-English population, perhaps because of basic humanity, or more likely due to the fact that much of the store's profit comes from that community. *That's business.* Yet, the store cannot take the chance of losing customers or other English-speaking employees because they find it too difficult to communicate with those limited in English. When an instructor comes onto the scene to teach those employees under a contract with the company, he or she may not fully understand the reasons behind the classes.

The person bringing the instructor in is not always well-versed in the goals; therefore, it is up to the instructor to question and investigate without forcing anyone to divulge any "company secrets." What I am referring to, if I may be so bold, is "double talk." Your instruction could be to teach the folks whatever they want to learn, just so their English gets better. *Excuse me, what do you mean by "better"?* you might ask. Though be sure to do so in more subtle terms. The response will likely be something along the lines of, "So that the employees can serve the customers and get along with the English-speaking employees better." Aha! That means that the employee needs customer and employee communication skills, not passing-the-TOEFL-test skills, or learning to communicate better in social situations. Though many communication skills cross over from one situation to another, your focus will need to be on the workplace. Your lessons should be structured based on workplace scenarios. What do we say when a customer approaches us? *How's it going, man?* or *May I help you, please?*

It is true that your sessions must tend to the needs of the students—but are those the needs as the company sees them? The student's deepest desire may be to learn English so that he or she can quit the store and go to college. That may also become your desire for that student, but it must be put on the back burner during the contract teaching time. Remember who is paying the light bill.

Churches can be great places to start up classes. The congregation may have a heart for the struggles of the limited-English folks in their neighborhood. And surely we would expect to find understanding and tolerance in such an environment. But wait just a minute: Remember who is paying the light bill . . . who is providing the facility . . . and who is paying your fine salary. What are the true reasons behind the English project? Is it to give local folk access to opportunity? Is it to give people the chance to become more familiar with the church in hope that they will then slip into services on Sunday? Is it to convert people? If it is the latter, then surely the classes should be taught by instructors trained in the teachings of that church, otherwise there is bound to be a doctrinal conflict. "But I'm not teaching religion," we quickly say. But . . . but . . . but you are teaching language, which is used to communicate ideas and ideals concerning life. People's perceptions are greatly influenced by their religious beliefs or lack thereof.

Many church programs are headed by individuals who are open-minded about other people's beliefs and very aware that people from other countries do not hold the same beliefs, even though they may belong to the same denominational organization. But then there are others who feel they are doing a disservice by allowing anything other than their own approaches to be utilized. It is necessary for you as instructor to feel out the situation. If there is any issue in question, be certain to discuss it with the folks with whom you are contracting.

The same principles hold when you are working with small private groups or with individuals. If they are paying you directly, then it is absolutely necessary that you have an ongoing conversation about what they expect and need. They, in a sense, are "paying the light bill." There will be times when what they think they need and what you think they need are two different things. "I want to learn slang!" they might tell you. And they need to learn to understand what people are saying when less-than-standard English is used. But you will come to realize that the student first needs to learn the standard usage, then learn how the slang is derived from it. *Cha gonna go?* Sure, you need to tell folks what that means, but take them to the meaning by way of standard English *Are you going to go?* The "are" can be understood, and the "you going to" is slurred into "cha gonna." You will need to work a bit with the proper sentence structure in order to get to the slurs and slang. But your students said they are interested only in the slang. Good. Now your job is to help them understand that their pronunciation will be horrible if they simply try to pick up the sounds and attach a possible meaning. If they first learn the standard, then see how it is deteriorated, they will get a much better grasp of the meaning and they may even be able to sling some slang around without it sounding like a mockery.

The important point to remember is that you owe something to whoever is paying you, unless of course you are willing to teach for free. Pay close attention to what the benefactor is saying about his or her goals and interests, and take time to talk with that person about the needs and interests of the students.

Teaching in Other Countries

The most exciting challenge is that of traveling to another country to teach. Some people find themselves drawn to a particular country for various reasons, and others simply pick a country based on sketchy knowledge. It is important to know as much as possible about the country you've selected, and to have some contacts there and some sort of safety net in the event that the unexpected happens.

If you are tied in with a sponsoring organization (religious, governmental, business-related), you can ask for assistance in learning about the country. The ideal strategy is to take a trip to that country first to familiarize yourself with the culture and language. Then, be sure that everything is in place before you leave.

If you do not have any sort of sponsor or tie, then you must take care to be sure that you are receive assistance on the other end, when you arrive in the host country. A pre-trip is a good idea. But, if you are unable to visit the country first, it is essential that you have extensive conversations with people who have gone to the country, particularly people who have taught there. You must speak with people from the school where you plan to teach and with people who are now teaching there. If you do not speak the language of that country, you must be certain that all communication is translated accurately. I would suggest that you do not rely fully on a written contract. Make sure that you also have an oral understanding (through good translation) of the terms of the contract.

**You will be surprised to find that
"comfortable accommodations"
vary greatly from one country to another.**

When you are teaching in another country, you will need to follow the plans that have been set in place by the people who are running the school. That will require a lot of flexibility on your part. Just take it easy, and give yourself time to absorb the culture and come to an understanding of why people do what they do.

Finding jobs in other countries can be an adventure. If you do not already have contacts or a position to walk into, then you might want to go to the internet. You will find yourself spending hours (or maybe days) surfing through the sites on international ESL jobs. Begin by searching English as a second language, teaching English in other countries, or teaching English internationally. You will be astounded at your findings. You may need to follow some links to get to the job listings, but don't give up -- they are out there. You can also find sites on which you can post your resume. You may be shocked to receive a good number of job offers quickly. Some countries are searching continuously for possible candidates. Many of the job listings mention qualifications, often what is considered to be their "wish list." They wish you had a master's degree in TESOL or something similar. They wish for extensive experience. But you may be surprised to find that you are pursued even though you do not have the qualifications listed.

What they really want, in most cases, is someone who can actually do the job of teaching people to speak English. It behooves you to take heed of your own safety in foreign countries. Be sure that you educate yourself by talking to many people about these issues. Try doing a search for "Teaching Abroad" and you might stumble upon new websites and information about the US government's stance on safety issue and travel in the area. Talk to people continuously and learn everything that you can until you feel good about your plans. The issues of professionalism carry over from one country to another. There are, however, some significant differences in perception from country to country. You should find people you can trust to help you weed through the perceptual differences.

TESOL Technology

The internet and other forms of technology are affecting the lives of many people, and that certainly includes the realm of education. Language can be acquired to some degree and strengthened when a person interacts with a CD or an online program. There are limitations due to the fact that the electronic program can only simulate real-life situations. Nevertheless, the language exercises can prepare the learners for real-life practice.

Many of the textbooks now come with CDs and even online accompaniments, and those can be quite effective. The trick is to learn how to use them and show your students how they can gain the most benefit from them. Do not be afraid of technology, and do not fear that it is going to take away your job. Use it to complement your work. Here are some samples of technology aids and how to use them:

- CDs—Use those that come with textbooks to extend your classroom teaching.

Use them to in EFL situations where the students' access to English-speaking people is limited. Use them as homework to reinforce lessons. Create your own CDs directly from your lessons by simply setting up an audio system and recording the lesson.

- Online quizzes and exams—Create quizzes in an online platform such that your students can access them from their computers. They can test themselves to get a better grasp of the area in which they need more study and practice. Create online comprehensive exams that act as a placement device. Create online comprehensive exams that act as pre- and post-assessments. Your students can test themselves before a course and after a course, and you can use the results to measure progress.

- Online lessons—Some free lessons can be accessed on the internet, and you can create your own online exercises and give your student access to them.

- Online courses—Several teaching companies have produced online courses, and students probably know more about them their teachers do. But, they usually are aware of the limitation of simulated practice. You needn't view those programs as competition to your teaching, but you can encourage students to spend their money wisely and to make certain that they are getting the foundation and building blocks necessary to solid language acquisition.

- DVDs—Videos and movies make for great fun and high interest in the classroom. Always play it safe and preview anything before showing it in class. Make certain that the content is acceptable for your students, and be sure that that it fits well into your lesson. Create videos and use them to show role-playing. If you have the proper equipment, you can project the video onto a large screen for easy viewing.

- Computer language programs—Some interesting strides have been made with language programs, and it will serve you well to learn about them. Teachers as well as students can learn from them. You might be able to get a free sample CD from one of the better-known programs, and you can examine it for teaching techniques.

It is important to recognize that writers and publishers have put in time and expense to producing such products as language-learning CDs and language programs. Be respectful by using them only with Fair Usage Laws of copyrights. In other words, never make copies of copyrighted materials, including CDs and DVDs, and hand them out to students.

Also, it is essential that your students have the technology in their homes to use CDs, DVDs, or internet programs, or that they have access to equipment in the school or at a nearby library.

Protecting Your Materials

As you teach and design courses, take precautions to protect your work. You can copyright your curricula (courses of study), lesson plans, and any other materials that you originate yourself. Over time you will build up a supply that will help you and probably others. If you originate you own material, copyright it. If you happen to create a particularly effective teaching tool, be sure to have it patented. That is an exciting element of creative teaching: that you have the opportunity to develop teaching materials and tools. They now belong to you, for use and for profit. Enjoy your teaching and use it to explore life and the world.

Appendix A: ESL Lesson Observation Protocol Form

(This form may be used to each time you observe an ESL or EFL classroom. It is to be completed after the observation, and it is in no way a criticism of the teacher, the classroom, or the school. It is a tool for the observer to sharpen his or her skills in the recognizing the effective techniques for language acquisition.)

Classlevel_____Location_____

Schedule_____ Observer _____

Activity	effective	vague	absent
introduction			
classroom management			
time management			
meaningful activity			
comprehensible input			
scaffolding of vocabulary and concepts			
assessment/review			
wrap up			

Balance of language components	low	high	balanced
listening			
speaking			
reading			
writing			

Affective domain	effective	moderate	problematic
reduced anxiety			
positive attitude			
increased motivation			

Comments: _____

_____

Appendix B: Course Worksheet

(This form should be used each time you develop a new course. Use it as a preliminary worksheet in order to consider what sort of course you are developing and what should be the objectives.)

Course Worksheet

Course type and level: _____

Description and goal:

_____
_____
_____
_____
_____
_____

Frequency and duration of sessions: _____

Course Objectives: By the time the students finish this course they should be able to:

_____
_____
_____
_____
_____
_____
_____

Appendix C: Course Development Template

(This form is helpful as you develop a course.)

ESL/EFL/ESOL Curriculum Development Template

Course title: _____

Class level: _____
_____
_____
_____
_____

Course description: _____
_____
_____
_____
_____

Instructor:_____**Location**:_____

Required text: _____

Schedule: _____ (frequency and duration of sessions)

Course Outcomes:

The participant will—

- demonstrate knowledge of _____
  _____

- demonstrate skills in _____
  _____

- gain understanding of _____
  _____

Course Requirements:

1. Attendance requirement _____
   _____

2. Class participation _____
   _____

3. Portfolio requirement _____
   _____

Course Calendar

Session 1—Lesson title: _____
Topics: _____
_____

Assignments: _____
_____

Assessment/review: _____
_____

Session 2—Lesson title: _____

Topics: _____

_____

Assignments: _____

_____

Assessment/review: _____

Session 3—Lesson title: _____

Topics: _____

_____

Assignments: _____

_____

Assessment/review: _____

Session 4—Lesson title: _____

Topics: _____

_____

Assignments: _____

_____

Assessment/review: _____

Session 5—Lesson title: _____

Topics: _____

_____

Assignments: _____

_____

Assessment/review: _____

Session 6—Lesson title: _____

Topics: _____

_____

Assignments: _____

_____

Assessment/review: _____

Session 7—Lesson title: _____

Topics: _____

_____

Assignments: _____

_____

Assessment/review: _____

Session 8—Lesson title: _____

Topics: _____

_____

Assignments: _____

_____

Assessment/review: _____

Session 9—Lesson title: _____

Topics: _____

_____

Assignments: _____

_____

Assessment/review: _____

Session 10—Lesson title: _____

Topics: _____

_____

Assignments: _____

_____

Assessment/review: _____

Session 11—Lesson title: _____

Topics: _____

_____

Assignments: _____

_____

Assessment/review: _____

Session 12—Lesson title: _____

Topics: _____

_____

Assignments: _____

_____

Assessment/review: _____

Appendix D: Lesson Plan Rubric

(This form is helpful as you develop your lesson plan.)

ESL Lesson Rubric

Lesson Developer _____

Class level_____

Number of students_____

Schedule_____

Objectives for language and content	1. 2. 3. 4.	
	Time and Activity	
Introduction		
Presentation		
Practice		

Performance	
Wrap-up	
Evidence of learning outcomes (how the objectives are demonstrated)	
1. 2. 3. 4	

Explanation of the use of strategies:

Classroom management	
Anxiety reduction	
Balance of components of Language (listening, speaking, reading, writing)	
Meaningful activity	
Comprehensible input	
Scaffolding	
Increase motivation	
Review/assessment	

Appendix E: Grammar Sites

(These sites contain information for incorporating grammar into your lessons, whether your teach grammar explicitly or implicitly.)

1. Owl Purdue Online Writing Lab: English Grammar. http://owl.english.purdue.edu/owl/section/1/5/

   This site contains the basics of grammar and can be used as a refresher for teachers.

2. Owl Purdue Online Writing Lab: ESL Instructors and Tutors. http://owl.english.purdue.edu/owl/section/5/24/

   This site contains resources to help teachers develop curricula for teaching writing to English language learners. There is also an ESL Orientation for Writing Lab and additional ESL teacher resources.

3. Using English.com: English Language Learning. http://www.usingenglish.com/

   This site contains English grammar quizzes and tests, lessons and handouts for teachers and students.

4. Ohio University Department of Linguistics. "English Grammar" & "ESL Student Resources." http://www.ohio.edu/linguistics/esl/grammar/index.html

   This site contains a collection of student resources for listening, speaking, reading and writing.

5. "Learning English with Professor Grammar" and related videos. http://www.youtube.com/watch?v=ySnT_5IcWGg&feature=related

   This site contains videos on grammar and link to additional videos.

6. "Helpful ESL Handouts from Susan Watson," http://sites.google.com/site/esl-helpfulhandouts/

   This site contains lesson handouts.

7. The Sounds of American English: http://www.uiowa.edu/~acadtech/phonetics/english/frameset.html

   This site contains audio bites of the sounds of English along with identification of the manner, place, and voice of articulation.

CPSIA information can be obtained at www.ICGtesting.com
Printed in the USA
LVOW02s2148200314

378332LV00008B/146/P

4384208